THE COTSWOLD MALE VOICE CHOIR 1949–2009

MALCOLM WILLIAMS

T0347002

The
History
Press

First published 2009
Reprinted 2020

The History Press
97 St George's Place, Cheltenham,
Gloucestershire, GL50 3QB
www.thehistorypress.co.uk

British Library Cataloguing in Publication Data.
A catalogue record for this book is available from the British Library.

ISBN 978 0 7524 5006 3

Typesetting and origination by The History Press
Printed in Great Britain by TJ International Ltd, Padstow, Cornwall.

Contents

Royalty payments to the Choir for this book
will help support their performances for other
charities.

Foreword

by BRIAN BLESSED

Honorary President
The Cotswold Male Voice Choir

When the Cotswold Male Voice Choir invited me to become their Honorary President some years ago, I replied 'How can I possibly refuse?' This was not a casual decision. I admired their honesty when they told me 'We can offer you nothing in return!' This forthright approach took me back to my upbringing in a Yorkshire mining community, where there was little patience for beating around the bush. I remembered the pride with which Yorkshire communities regarded their local choir. Like their local football team, they expected high standards but they would be fiercely loyal.

Since my 'elevation' to Honorary President, I have maintained an interest in what the Choir has achieved. I never cease to be amazed by the amount of money and the hours of rehearsal time each member invests without a thought for any personal gain. Perhaps that is not totally true, because I suspect their motivation is the pride they feel every time they step out on stage, knowing that their concerts are supporting good causes and helping other people. This restores my faith in human nature when we hear so much about today's 'me' culture.

They obviously enjoy the singing and the camaraderie. If not, the Choir would not still be performing after sixty years, and this shines through in the quality of their singing. To any man who is thinking about singing, go along to one of the Choir's rehearsals to see how it all comes together. You will experience a warm welcome and you can share in their pride.

To all the members of the Cotswold Male Voice Choir, I say 'Terrific work, keep it up and, just because I may not be there with you, don't think I'm not keeping an eye on you!'

Acknowledgements

Profound gratitude to the commissioning editors, Claire Forbes, Nicola Guy and David Lewis of The History Press. Special thanks to Steve Allsup for his unstinting help, support and encouragement, and also to Carole Allsup for her secretarial expertise, and Paul Hipkiss.

Specific thanks to Don Baker, Dave Ford and Colin Francis for their detailed input, and appreciation for the members who generously shared their photographs, memorabilia and anecdotes of the Choir's sixty year history. Fond thoughts also of the probably countless singers, many of whom also served faithfully in administration as chairmen, secretaries, treasurers, librarians and stage managers. Hallowed are the musical directors, accompanists and soloists whose words and notes will always resonate.

Above all, we salute all the lovely, venerated ladies who have helped, supported and inspired their men-folk for six decades, without complaint, and with no thought of reward, in the sacred cause of music.

> Her brood gone from her;
> And her thoughts as still
> As the waters under a ruined mill...

Malcolm Williams
2009

PART ONE

1949-1977

A VOICE FROM THE VALLEYS

If you sing fortissimo, people will hear you.
If you sing pianissimo, people will listen to you.

Dave Williams

The genesis of the Cotswold Male Voice Choir must be synonymous with its founder conductor, Dave Williams. I make this claim not only because he was my father, but because I think of him as being the father of this choir.

Born into a large music loving family of anthracite-coal miners in Swansea Valley in 1913, Dave fitted the familiar adage, 'To be born Welsh is to be born with music in the blood and poetry in the soul.' A gifted singer and pianist, he once won first prize as a juvenile competitor in the open pianoforte solo class at a Welsh Eisteddfod. Parlour singers were plentiful; Dave was ever in demand as a natural yet shy accompanist.

At age fourteen he left school in order to work down the pit, first as a coal hewer, finally as a colliery examiner underground. He worked alongside his father, a collier for forty years. The brutal life of a pick and shovel worker was hazardous. Dave suffered the horror of witnessing a 'butty' being crushed by a roof fall. Pit ponies could be companions as well as kindred workers in the darkness.

The Smiths Male Voice choir logo.

But, for the sensitive musician, music was neither diminished nor dimmed. Tough, scarred miners descending a vertical shaft in a cage to toil at a coal seam were resolutely united as they gently harmonised the appropriate hymn 'Lead kindly light amid the encircling gloom...' After being nursed for diphtheria in an isolation hospital, Dave was invalided out of the coal field, obliging him to leave the valleys in 1945. Finding engineering work in Cheltenham (a veritable culture shock) he was joined by his family in 1946, settling at the Smiths factory in Bishop's Cleeve. As a precision engineer, then as a time-and-motion-study engineer, he was at the heartbeat of Smiths, many of his numerous colleagues becoming close friends, some of them later becoming fellow singers. Lathes and laughter led to harmony on the shop floor. The prospect of a choir somehow seemed inevitable.

Consumed by music, Dave combined his love of carpentry (self-taught) with his passion for upright and grand pianos. He restrung, restored and even restructured them. How he actually shortened one grand piano may always remain a mystical puzzle, but perfect pitch and a wide-ranging singing voice served him admirably as a self-taught piano tuner.

The Smiths Male Voice Choir EP Spindle Label.

Feeling 'exiled' from his beloved Wales and its rich musical heritage, especially the venerable traditions of male voice singing, he conceived the idea of forming a male choir in his workplace. The gradual gestation period resulted in the birth of the Smiths Male Voice Choir. This was preceded by informal lunchtime machine shop meetings of a small, dedicated coterie of employees united by the joy of singing. Eventually, spontaneous discussions culminated in a formal general meeting held in the works' canteen of S Smith & Sons (England) Ltd at the Bishop's Cleeve site on 11 May 1949 at 5.30 p.m.

The agenda specified 'for the purpose of forming a male voice choir'. Eighteen persons attended, Mr Arthur Jones officiating as Chairman. Proposed and accepted, three of the founding fathers were elected; Ken Eldridge, Hon. Treasurer; Jack Williams, Hon. Secretary and, unrelated, Dave Williams as 'Party Conductor'. Each member contributed sixpence per week for the purposes of sheet music, etc.

On 19 May a second meeting of eighteen persons ratified the inauguration of the Choir. Gwynne Jenkins was appointed Chairman; Arthur Jones became debut accompanist and A. Carr was librarian. From that seminal little machine shop, music was already following in the first three pieces of TTBB arrangements ordered by the Choir:

23 copies of 'Smiling Through' at 1s per copy
24 copies of 'Passing By' at 4d per copy
24 copies of 'The Jolly Roger' at 6d per copy

This was duly invoiced to Mr M.A. Lulham at 'Sports and Social', plus an application to the general executive for a 'grant of money' payable to the emergent male voice choir funds. Initially, the officially allocated practice was Thursday from 5.15 p.m.–7.25 p.m. In later years, Wednesday rehearsal became the choir tradition. It was held in the works' canteen, well staged and equipped for public performances, when pantomimes and kindred amateur dramatics attracted big audiences.

With characteristic modesty, Dave Williams accepted identity as fledgling Musical Director as temporary, 'until someone else took over'. That was to take another twenty-eight years! Early on, sectional rehearsals were held at home, by rotation, tenors and basses combining in general practice. Several Welsh members, like Dave, had imported their *hwyl* and *hiraeth*, two words almost impossible to translate from Welsh; spirit, and yearning for the native land. Membership was drawn from all four home countries, but restricted to Smiths employees at first.

Concurrently, Dave also formed the Smiths Ladies Choir, some members related to Smiths Male Voice Choir, including Dave's daughter. This resulted in some joint concerts, styles contrasting as a kind of cross-fertilisation in music. May Rees, of the Ladies Choir, had four brothers, John, David, Bryn and Alan, all tenors in the Male Voice Choir. In the popular BBC radio show 'Workers' Playtime', May sang the soprano solo 'Softly as in a Morning Sunrise', accompanied by Dave Williams, in the canteen.

The Smiths Choir.

The factory's family ambience, supportive in adversity, was typified in the pride and support of management, especially Messrs. Lulham, Watson and, above all, the site resident Director, Mr Ben Haviland.

An enthusiastic champion of the male choir, he jubilantly ended one concert by donating a cheque for fifty guineas 'out of my own pocket' to the Choir; extreme generosity in 1950! Also, for some time, one of the Choir Honorary Presidents was Sir Ralph-Gordon Smith.

Steadily developing its own distinctive voice, the Choir concentrated on pitch, diction and a pleasing mellow tone. It grew in membership and in an eclectic repertoire of TTBB arrangements of spirituals, hymns, operas, shanties, anthems and, of course, traditional male voice favourites beloved of music festival competitions. Gradually more light-hearted songs were introduced, like hits from popular musicals, achieving a more balanced programme.

Bennington Hall, Cheltenham, for St. David's Day celebrations yesterday evening.

They were members of the S. Smith and Sons (England), Ltd., Male Voice Choir, with their leader, Mr. David Williams. Mr. Arthur Jones, of Bishop's Cleeve, was pianist.

Their repertoire was large. Songs included "Fishermen of England" (Montague Phillips), "Soldiers' Chorus" (Gounod), "Smilin' Thro'" (Arthur Penn), "Passing By" (Edward Purcell), and "Bless This House" (Brahe). The last three pieces were arranged by Doris Arnold.

Mr. W. G. Griffiths and Mr. G. Jenkins sang two duets, "The Gendarmes" (Offenbach) and "If I Can Help Somebody." Both sang solos. "Calon Lan," a solo number, was sung by Master Malcolm Williams.

MONOLOGUE FUN

Paul Buckley, with his accordion, played the tunes of popular songs, and the large audience joined lustily in community singing. Mr. J. Williams's monologue, "How we saved the Barge" caused a great deal of fun.

Mrs. C. Richards (contralto) sang "The Holy City," with Miss Freda Burrows (pianist), while Mrs. W. M. King accompanied herself in two songs "Good Night" and "Mentra Gwen" ("Dearest Gwen").

The chairman throughout the evening was Mr. Arthur Jones, of Cheltenham.

Two Welshmen, who live in Cheltenham, Brig. W. G. Hewett and Mr. David Lewis, proposed and seconded votes of thanks to the choir.

This happy, informal concert, which was organised by the Cheltenham Cymrodorion (Welsh Society) ended with the singing of "God Save the King" and "Hen Wlad Fy Nhadau" ("Land of my Fathers").

SMITHS' CHOIR IN VARIETY CONCERT

An enjoyable concert was arranged by the male voice choir of S. Smith and Sons (England) Ltd. on Friday, at the work's canteen.

Members of the choir excelled themselves with their well-planned programme.

They sang several groups of songs from a versatile repertoire including "The Soldier's Dream," "When Evening's Twilight," and by special request "The Happy Wanderer."

The audience gave them an enthusiastic reception.

Johnny Walker, the well known ventriloquist and "Ozzy" caused much hilarity.

Dorothy Allan charmed everyone with her clear soprano voice, and her choice of romantic songs.

"Steveen," the magician, enthralled with his magic. Without a word he produced watches from nowhere and made other things disappear just as easily.

Michael Jenkins aged 14, played two piano solos "The Avalanche," and Chopin's Waltz in D Flat.

The "Merry Moniks" dressed as Hill Billies formed an amusing comedy harmonica quartet.

Mr. David Williams, the conductor, can be justly proud of the success of this concert.

Mr. Cyril Cox the compere thanked Mr. Allan Adams, the accompanist who had filled a gap caused by the illness of the usual accompanist.

He also thanked the electricians and "back room boys" for their assistance.

Members of the management who attended included Mr. and Mrs. Ben Haviland and Mr. W. Watson.

Pictured with his wife, Mr Ben Haviland, Resident Director of S. Smith & Sons, Bishop's Cleeve, early 1950s.

Cotswold Male Voice Choir – then S. Smith and Sons (England) Ltd Male Voice Choir. Early formal photograph of choir members from 1954. Included in the 1954 complement (back row, fourth from left) is a youthful Don Baker, also shown on a 2008 group photograph at the end of this book, but rather less youthful! The 'founding fathers' are clearly pictured.

The Smiths Male Voice Choir membership, as at the AGM on 9 June 1954 was Mr A. Adams (Pianist), Mr D. Baker, Mr F. Beagley (Librarian), Mr K. Bruton, Mr A. Carr (Chairman), Mr C. Cox (Compère and Publicity), Mr E. Crisp, Mr D. Davies, Mr L. Davies, Mr F. Dean, Mr R. Dimond, Mr J. Dowsett, Mr K. Eldridge, Mr A. Ewing, Mr T. Febery, Mr F. Gibbons, Mr W. Griffiths, Mr J. Haggett, Mr W. Jarvis, Mr G. Jenkins, Mr H. McCullum, Mr I. Morgan, Mr A. Perrey (Treasurer), Mr D. Rees, Mr I Rees, Mr G. Salter, Mr D. South, Mr N. Tansley (Secretary), Mr G. Wilkins, Mr I.D. Williams, Mr J. Williams, Mr M.D. Williams (Conductor).

Always there were talented soloists within the Choir, as well as excellent guest artistes.

Concert venues throughout the Cotswolds replaced the old canteen stage. Early performances in village schools, halls and churches extended to colleges, cathedrals and town halls outside the county, reaching Worcestershire, Wiltshire, Somerset and Devon. But in the '50s and '60s the Choir was committed to the culture of competition singing. Its ethos was always to make music, bring pleasure to audiences and raise funds in support

Certificate of Merit awarded in a choral competition, 1958.

The Choir competing in the 'home town' choral competition.

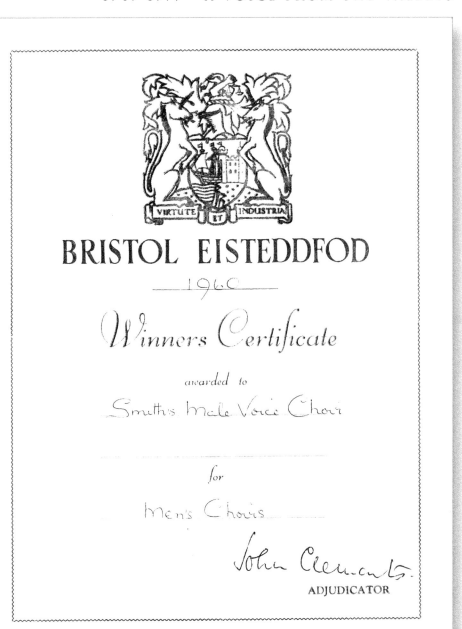

Winner's certificate at Bristol Eisteddfod, 1960.

TEWKESBURY CONCERT AIDS RED CROSS

Some excellent choral singing, monologues, vocal and piano solos and a sketch formed the ingredients of an extremely entertaining variety concert given by Smiths' Male Voice Choir at the Watson Hall, Tewkesbury, last night.

The concert was in aid of the British Red Cross Society (Tewkesbury Division) funds, and the choir gave their services.

The Mayor of Tewkesbury (Ald. T. G. Bannister), who was accompanied by the Mayoress, paid tribute to the work of the Red Cross in war and peace.

"In the past four or five months, since I became Mayor, I have been astounded at the enormous number of people giving their time and services gladly and freely for their fellow men," he commented, in praising the work of the B.R.C.S. and other voluntary organisations.

The choir, conducted by Mr. D. Williams, quickly proved their merit with a fine rendering of "Rose of England" (Novello), which they followed with the Serenade from the "Fair Maid of Perth."

They received a fine reception for their Stephen Foster medley, which included such old favourites as "My Old Kentucky Home," "Louisiana Belle," and others. Other items included "Comrades in Arms," "Whiffenpoof Song," the "Soldiers' Chorus," "Love, Could I Only Tell Thee," and "Laudamis." The accompanist was Mr. L. Holland.

Jack Williams presented a monologue, "A Hole in the Road," and a fake "audition" carried out by five members of the choir proved equally funny.

Solos were sung by D. Rowe, H. McCullen, and G. Jenkins, while Reg Diamond gave his hilarious version of "Devonshire Dialect."

The programme was compered by Mr. J. Parker.

of nominated charities. But the competition stage imposed its own demanding discipline.

EXTRA DISCIPLINE

In the world of set pieces, the Choir rehearsed and performed a variety of songs at competitive festivals in Bristol, Birmingham, Swindon, Cowley and Cheltenham, enjoying considerable success in the Under 40 Voices, the Open, Under 70 Voices and Gold Cup Classes. Certificates for Merit and Distinction were excelled by Winners Class triumphs at the Bristol Eisteddfod, both in 1960 and 1963. As well as winning the Rose Bowl in Swindon, the Choir also brought home from Bristol the Winner's Shield. It was clutched and strummed like a harp, by the jubilant Secretary, Lyn Badge, during the homeward bus journey to Cheltenham that night!

Some of the adjudicators remarks confirmed the good health of the Choir; comments included 'good blend', 'exemplary chording', 'excellent attack', 'well-drilled male voice choralism', 'an exciting performance', 'a lovely tone', and 'I congratulate you on your achievement chorally'. Great credit to a relatively small choir competing against much bigger choirs and earning the Distinction mark of eighty-nine for that great 'war horse', The Crusaders! Such was the wisdom of eminent adjudicators such as John Tobin, John Clements and the great Herbert Howells.

Undoubtedly, the discipline and formality of competitive singing proved invaluable, but it required precious rehearsal time devoted to the intense practice of a few set pieces, mostly never to be sung again. The Choir withdrew from the competition arena in order

Echo cutting. Red Cross variety concert at Watson Hall, Tewkesbury.

to concentrate on the expanding repertoire and general stage deportment.

Inaugural members wore dark suits augmented by badged blazers liveried with the logo SMVC, ties being gradually replaced by bow ties. The art of 'a true gentleman always tying his own bow tie' eluded one 1954 member, frustrated as his bow tie wriggled like a trout at his throat. He resigned from the Choir but was later re-instated, presumably, as one wag quipped 'once he'd mastered his troublesome bow tie'.

At that time the Choir imposed a 1s fine for absenteeism on its thirty-five members; and sheet copies were banned during concert performances, a habit never to be broken. Sweepstake ticket sales raised income for the general fund; a Tonic Scale Chart was used in learning sessions; a tape recorder (state of the art then) was purchased for rehearsals too.

Sartorial requirements changed. Dark lounge suits were under threat. One choir member - a top tenor naturally - appeared in concert wearing a black dinner jacket. Sacrilege or epiphany? Well, the idea 'caught on', black dinner jackets becoming the official concert dress, without coercion. Bow ties remained a bickering point, first black, then maroon, then blue. Hardly haute couture but the black dinner jacket and white dress shirt endured as the convention, this formal attire creating an air of Castilian elegance on stage, another meaning to the catchphrase 'Men in Black'.

By now a non-employee of Smiths had joined the Choir - another top tenor naturally - unsettling another convention. That too 'caught on', so that new members from diverse demographies widened the scope of recruitment. The family style of fellowship generated an enviable quality of camaraderie. This proved infectious when associating with other choirs in the UK and Europe. The Choir fraternity had stamped its abiding hallmark.

Echo cutting. RAFA annual town hall concert, Battle of Britain week, a Choir 'fixture'.

THE MAYOR'S PLEA FOR R.A.F.A.

The large audience which attended the Dedication and Concert given by the Royal Air Forces' Association in the Town Hall, Cheltenham, last night augurs well for the success of this year's Battle of Britain week.

Before the concert began the Mayor of Cheltenham, Coun. A. W. Mann, reminded the audience of the debt owed by everyone to the Royal Air Force and the opportunity of repaying that debt by supporting the Royal Air Forces' Association.

Following the Mayor's speech the Rev. D. G. Thomas, chaplain to the local R.A.F.A. branch, led the entire assembly in prayers of dedication.

Prominent among the programme's many excellent items was the Cotswold Symphony Orchestra under the capable baton of Major Charles Lambert. They showed a high degree of skill right from the first rousing notes of "The Royal Air Force March" to the "Land of Hope and Glory" finale.

The rest of their programme consisted of the "Mikado" overture, the waltz from "Der Rosenkavalier" and a selection from "La Boutigue Fantasque."

Smiths' Male Voice Choir earned loud and prolonged applause with a smooth and well-trained presentation of six songs. Soprano Doreen Bissell sang a selection of well chosen numbers in a most pleasing and natural manner.

Vincento Celetano, tenor, sang a number of operatic arias with great competence. He was the only one among the soloists who is a serving airman, being at present stationed at R.A.F. Innsworth.

Some delightful works of Chopin were played by Gordon McNee.

The evening's entertainment was rounded off with an address by Mr. J. Bennett, who urged the public to support the R.A.F.A. to the best of their ability and to give generously during the coming week.

A silver collection realised a total of just under £50.

CORONATION CONCERT AT BISHOP'S CLEEVE

The Male Voice Choir of S. Smith & Son's (Eng.) Ltd., gave a delightful concert in the factory canteen at Bishop's Cleeve, last evening.

The programme was varied and included typically English songs by the choir, with solo pieces and comic interpretations.

The choir was introduced by Mr. Cyril Cox and we were taken into the realms of Elizabethan England by the song "Elizabeth of England." Mr. W Griffiths and Mr. Gwyn Jenkins both rendered solos and it was a pleasure to listen to their robust tenor voices. Paul Buckley transported the audience on a flight of fancy to Continental cafes with his gay accordion playing. Miss Gillian Harvey, who has a charming soprano voice, sang simple English songs.

Three members of the choir added to the evening's enjoyment (Mr J. Williams, Mr. K. Eldridge, Mr. E. Crisp) with a sketch entitled "Three Old Maids." Miss Nannette Price, who is eight years old, and was dressed in a patriotic outfit, made a fairylike ballerina and a clever little tap dancer.

The Male Voice Choir had invited the newly formed Ladies' Choir to show the progress they had made, and in the second part of the programme they were introduced by Mr. M A. Lulham and sang two songs, "The Barcarole" and "Count Your Blessings." The blending of their voices was very pleasant. The Male Voice Choir's rendering of " Rose of England " was especially enjoyed. The guest artist, Jack Avis, gave us the benefit of his wide experience as a comedian, and his American-style humour was fully appreciated.

The finale was a spirited rendering of " Land of Hope and Glory " by the combined choirs. Mr. D. Williams, the conductor, is to be congratulated on his successful training of both the Ladies' and Male Voice Choirs. Mr. L. Holland, the accompanist, also deserves special mention. Mr. Ben Haviland (Resident Director, S. Smith & Son's) and Mrs. Haviland, attended.

A concert to celebrate the Queen's Coronation, 1953.

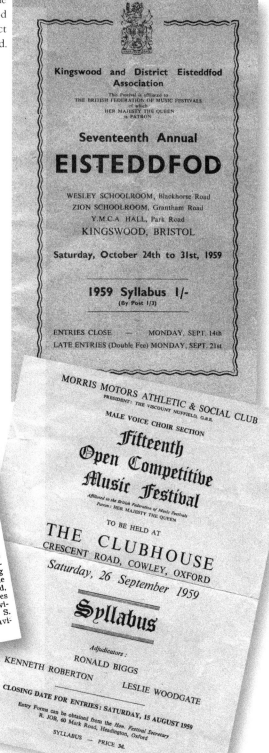

Programme from Kingswood and District Eisteddfod.

Kingswood and District Eisteddfod Association

This Festival is affiliated to
THE BRITISH FEDERATION OF MUSIC FESTIVALS
of which
HER MAJESTY THE QUEEN
is PATRON

Seventeenth Annual

EISTEDDFOD

WESLEY SCHOOLROOM, Blackhorse Road
ZION SCHOOLROOM, Grantham Road
Y.M.C.A. HALL, Park Road
KINGSWOOD, BRISTOL

Saturday, October 24th to 31st, 1959

1959 Syllabus 1/-
(By Post 1/3)

ENTRIES CLOSE — MONDAY, SEPT. 14th
LATE ENTRIES (Double Fee) MONDAY, SEPT. 21st

MORRIS MOTORS ATHLETIC & SOCIAL CLUB
PRESIDENT: THE VISCOUNT NUFFIELD, G.B.E.

MALE VOICE CHOIR SECTION

Fifteenth
Open Competitive
Music Festival

Affiliated to the British Federation of Music Festivals
Patron : HER MAJESTY THE QUEEN

TO BE HELD AT

THE CLUBHOUSE
CRESCENT ROAD, COWLEY, OXFORD

Saturday, 26 September 1959

Syllabus

Adjudicators :
RONALD BIGGS
KENNETH ROBERTON
LESLIE WOODGATE

CLOSING DATE FOR ENTRIES: SATURDAY, 15 AUGUST 1959
Entry Forms can be obtained from the Hon. Festival Secretary
R. JOB, 60 Mark Road, Headington, Oxford
SYLLABUS — PRICE 3d.

Oxford Music Festival programme, 1959.

'She Walks in Beauty', the Choir at Dave Williams'
daughter's wedding, 1959.

Distinction certificate from
Cheltenham Spa Music Festival, 1961.

This warmth of fraternity tended to induce a matching response from audiences in hospitals (a regular Christmas venue), in hospices, care homes for the elderly, several visits to Gloucester prison (not as inmates!) and especially in one memorable concert in the grim maximum security prison in Bristol.

A CAPTIVE AUDIENCE

Just entering the prison was more than intimidating, stage fright reaching an unprecedented level. Performing in the crowded chapel, supervised by warders, the Choir gradually won over the hearts of the tense, flint-faced inmates, some of them 'lifers'. To the fervour and finesse of the singing was added a kind of radiance in such a gloomy place; men

Presentation to Jessie Gott, 12 December 1977. From left to right: Alan White, Dewi Davies, Ted Gough, Malcolm Williams, Ivor Attwood, Gwynne Jenkins and Phil Howells with Jessie.

singing together were communing with men doing penance together, a rare and special harmony amid discord. In a place of imprisonment, music still soared. The audience's initial scepticism and tentative applause changed to smiles and laughter, concluding in a rousing ovation and a demand for encores. Who could forget Fred Render's relaxed style of amusing monologues, helping to relax such a 'captive audience'. As ever, music claimed the final word - or note.

The stronghold of masculinity was eventually breached by a taciturn, undemonstrative north-country lady, Jessie Gott. Choir member Fred Gott persuaded his wife Jessie to accompany the choristers 'for a song or two'. Defiantly reluctant at first, Jessie agreed to help out the choir until a replacement accompanist was confirmed. Jessie stayed as confirmed accompanist - for the next eighteen years!

THE GENTLE TOUCH

Ladies have always been vital in the Choir's evolution. Ever supportive and reliable, they have helped, guided and inspired six decades of male singing. When 'the boys' are on stage, their ladies are metaphorically in the wings, waiting, watching - maybe sometimes wondering? Unsung heroines, they are priceless and, of course, tolerant. This book is dedicated to them. Bless them all.

Ladies Night was an annual and sacrosanct event following a favourite format; a formal dinner dance followed by 'mixed choir' singing. Sometimes, each lady discovered a personal gift amid the table place-settings, or even the surprise of seeing her partner making an unexpected cabaret appearance that had been rehearsed in secret. Tolerance again! And patience...

Much loved were the Choir's regular guest artistes, mostly contraltos and sopranos: Pepita Wishaw, Gillian Harvey, Eleanor Parker, Lesley Guy and most often and welcome, Enid Walklett, whose orbital notes in 'Where my Caravan...' may never land again. She graced the concert stage with her elegance and joyful singing, sometimes duetting with

SMITH'S MALE VOICE CHOIR

LADIES' NIGHT

ROYAL GEORGE HOTEL
BIRDLIP

Saturday 22nd March, 1952

Ladies Night programme, 1952.

SMITHS MALE VOICE CHOIR

PRESIDENT : RALPH GORDON-SMITH ESQ.

VICE-PRESIDENT'S : T.W.C. FISHER ESQ.

L.C. HARMAN ESQ.

AIR VICE MARSHALL S.N. WEBSTER
C.B.E., A.F.C., R.A.F. (Ret'd)

F. WORTHINGTON ESQ.

Part of a Ladies' Night programme, 1967.

Ladies Night at Cheltenham Racecourse, 1977.
Pete Wilkes, Mike Powell, Malcolm Williams, Dewi Davies, Alan Donnelly, Ted Gough, Charlie King, John Haggett and Harry Goodall with the ladies.

contralto Ruby or with her piano accompanist, Jean Lea. Jean later became an outstanding long-serving choir accompanist. The Painswick area was doubly blessed with the presence of two such musical and charming ladies. Yet at each Christmas raffle, a major source of choir income, there was no shortage of unofficial guest sopranos, wives and partners singing carols with unguessable skills, testing their men-folk, and perhaps even competing?

ANNIVERSARIES

The first significant choir anniversary was the celebration of year one in its history. This was commemorated by an inscribed barometer, ceremoniously presented to Dave Williams 'With Appreciation of the Members of Smiths Male Voice Choir. First Anniversary, May 1950'. Sixty years later that barometer still indicates 'Fair Weather'.

In May 1970, the Smiths Industries Men's Choir celebrated its 'coming of age' with a Twenty-First Anniversary Ladies Night, meaningful and enjoyable as always. Four years later this was followed by the formal Silver Jubilee celebrations, a dinner dance attended by Guests of Honour, The Mayor and Mayoress of Cheltenham (Councillor and Mrs D Martin-Jones) plus the Choir's President, Mr C.J.E. Hosegood and his wife. It was an evening of jubilation and nostalgia, with a flashback to that little factory machine shop from which dreams had manufactured a choir. A more tangible souvenir was a specially commissioned, inscribed plaque produced by the pottery at Prinknash Abbey. Each choir member was formally presented with a plaque, dated 1974. As normal, the hotel bar stayed open late, and the 'mixed

Cheltenham Welsh Society cutting, 1974.

CHELTENHAM WELSH SOCIETY CELEBRATION

About 85 members and friends of Cheltenham Welsh Society enjoyed their annual St. David's Day celebration, "Cinio Gwyl Dewi Sant" at the Queen's Hotel.

The chairman of the society, Mr. Harold Hughes, presided. He asked the company to rise, in memory of their late president, Mr. Gwyn Thomas, who died a few weeks previously.

After the loyal toast, and the "Prince of Wales and Land of my fathers," Mrs. Nan Williams, vice-president, called the register of the counties, a long-standing tradition.

Almost every Welsh county had its representative, and English, Scottish and Irish friends also stood in turn.

The guest speaker, Mr. David Martin-Jones, spoke of the love and veneration which the Welsh people hold for their patron saint. They gather together in places all over the world to remember their native land and traditions.

Wales, he said, has sent its people as exports to every other country, besides England, along with other valuable exports such as coal, iron, steel, silver and even gold; the stones at Stonehenge were the oldest of these, and the very earliest transport problem one can imagine.

The most important exports though, were the Welsh people, with their gifts of music, drama, the arts, and political activity. They would no doubt continue for a long time to enrich the life of the countries they lived in.

Mr. Martin-Jones was thanked on behalf of the society by Mrs. W. M. Keen, secretary. An hours entertainment by Smiths' Industries men's choir concluded a very happy evening.

Cheltenham Welsh Society programme, 1974.

Cymdeithas Gymraeg Cheltenham

CINIO DYDD
GWYL
DEWI SANT

GWEST'R FRENHINES
7.0 — 7.30 p.m.

NOS SADWRYN MAWRTH 2ail 1974
Tocyn £2.50

QUEEN'S HOTEL, CHELTENHAM

SATURDAY MARCH 2nd 1974
7.0 — 7.30 p.m.

Ticket £2.50

Cheltenham Welsh Society ticket, 1974.

Cheltenham and District Welsh Society

Cinio Gwyl Dewi Sant

Nos Sadwrn 28 Chwefron 1976
Saturday February 28th

Queen's Hotel, Cheltenham

7 for 7.30 p.m.

Tocyn - Ticket £3.00

choir' caroused happily – no competition singing that night!

WELSH EXILES

For many years the Choir maintained its strong cultural links with the Cheltenham Welsh Society, regularly providing musical entertainment at official functions. The Society's 'favourite choir' mastered some songs in Welsh especially for after-dinner music, the words rehearsed phonetically with the aid of Welsh-speaking members. The song 'Arabella', originally sung in English, was transformed when performed with the pride and passion of the Welsh 'Myfanwy', ever a favourite request with audiences everywhere. Dave Williams' wife Nan, as Vice-President, was always a heartbeat between the Society and the Choir.

Always essential, yet sometimes not lauded, piano accompanists were fundamental in the Choir's structure. Founder accompanist Arthur Jones had a son, Colin, whose membership is still remembered for his basso profundo voice, equalled in later years by the most modest of members, Arthur Bateman. Both singers seem to resonate in memory today – the magic of music. Eventually, Arthur Jones was succeeded by two other male accompanists, Allan Adams (who played memorable Chopin solos in Cheltenham Town Hall) and Lew Holland, whose son-in-law Colin Stillman sings with the Choir today. And then there was of course Jessie, the 'temporary accompanist', until her retirement in 1977.

Echo cutting. Dunnally Street School, PTA twenty-fifth anniversary.

SMITHS' CHOIR ENTERTAIN AT P.T.A. PARTY

The annual meeting and 25th birthday party of Dunally Street School Parent-Teacher Association was held at the school.

Miss F. L. Rowe, chairman of the P.T.A., introduced the meeting, which was well attended by staff and parents.

There were two vacancies on the committee, and Mrs. Russell and Mr. Beavins were elected. Mr. Adams and Mr. Kelly agreed to continue in office. After discussion on a suggested programme for next year, the business meeting closed.

The parents and staff then enjoyed a buffet supper, prepared by the refreshment committee and the parents of the children in class one, at the school.

The school managers were guests of the P.T.A. and Mrs. Brookes, wife of Hon. Alderman R. F. Brookes, cut the birthday cake given by Mr. Lloyd.

The school caretakers, Mr. and Mrs. G. Dix, have retired after many years of loyal and devoted service to the school. They were presented with a Teasmade by the P.T.A. in appreciation of their work.

After refreshments, the P.T.A. were entertained by Smiths' Industrial Male Voice Choir and their guest soprano, Mrs. Leslie Guy.

The programme was an interesting one and varied from negro spirituals to rousing Russian Songs.

CONCERT A BIG SUCCESS

A brass and choral concert given at the Town Hall, Cheltenham, was attended by a small but appreciative audience.

The brass consisted of the Burton Constructional Newhall Band, conducted by Ernest Woodhouse, who gave a wonderful performance, highlights being "Round the Horn", a tenor solo by Ralph Blackett, an arrangement of "Jolson Memories", and many other well-known band arrangements.

The final band item was an exhilarating performance of "Hootenanny", and the audience insisted on an encore.

The choral part of the evening was provided by the combined voices of Smiths' Industries Male Voice Choir and the Gloucestershire Police Choir, conducted by Mr. D. Williams and accompanied by Mr. Andrew Downie.

This was an excellent performance by 80 voices, all their items being well received, especially "Kalinka" with soloist G. Morran.

The audience participation in the final item, a rendering by the band and choir of "Jesus Shall Reign", to the tune Rimmington, provided a splendid ending to an enjoyable musical evening, ably produced and compered by Mr. Jack Beckingham.

P.D.B.

Echo cutting. Brass and choral concert, combined choirs 'in fraternity'.

THE 'AFTERGLOW'

Informal, spontaneous singing was ever a characteristic of the Choir. Concert engagements didn't end on stage. Afterwards, in nearby hotels or inns, relaxed, lubricated singers performed an 'après-concert', the 'secondary performance' or, the more popularly known 'afterglow'. Amazing how profundo a bass could descend, how high tenors could soar with the inspiration of alcohol. As the ale flowed inhibitions dried up. Soloists who confidently volunteered to sing opera arias in a public house didn't necessarily partner the 'fervour' with the 'finesse'! But, if musical precision sagged, bar sales always ascended.

Perhaps the most memorable and beloved venue for an 'afterglow' was the thatched King's Head Inn, Bishop's Cleeve, hosted by landlord and landlady, Dave and Mary Davies. They effectively adopted the Choir, accommodating thirsty singers after local concerts and after every Wednesday night rehearsal. Dave and Mary hospitably prepared sustenance, their 'back room' almost a chapel for choir worship, with fine acoustics, especially by Advent candlelight. For years, committee meetings and even some AGMs were held there. Fun to speculate how many new members were unexpectedly recruited as a result of 'strangers' overhearing an afterglow. Irrespective of location, throughout its history the Choir has bonded its fraternity in the unity of music. An old saying was never truer than this in a choir context: 'There are no strangers here, only friends we haven't yet met.'

The informal/unofficial singers frequenting The King's Head Inn attracted the nickname, 'King's Head Chorale'. 'Devout' singers included unforgettable local characters like Harold 'Page Eight' Price, whose funeral wake was held at this inn after a memorable and moving church service at St Michael and All Angels, Bishop's Cleeve, where several choir concerts were staged. Also, there was the irreplaceable 'Brewery Bill' Brunsdon, of 'Cider Drinker Song' fame who, eventually, found his favourite 'Gold Mine in the Sky'.

Occasionally, extra-curricular instincts were disciplined, as exemplified at a Choir dinner-dance Christmas party, held at the Gupshill Manor, Tewkesbury in December 1975. Conventional entertainment was augmented by a surprise cabaret, the barber shop quintet of Mike Powell, Aled Williams, Alan Gilkes, Harold Price and Malcolm Williams. Carefully

Choir mascot 'Amadeus', ever a keen fan of the 'afterglow', pictured at home in his favourite chair. At formal concerts, 'Amadeus' always sat on top of the piano! Although retired now, he had a special provenance, prone to abduction!

and secretly rehearsed in each other's homes, 'The Unfab Five' (no threat to the Fab Four) performed, unaccompanied, 'Don't Let The Rains Come Down' and 'I'll Stay Single'. Delighted ovation was climaxed by the Musical Director buying the Unfab Five a round of drinks. Wow!

BOYS AT PLAY

Choir social life was in harmony with the music. A favourite and much anticipated event was the members' annual coach outing, usually to the seaside, singing providing an accompaniment to relaxation. With the noblest intentions, 'the boys' sometimes blundered into unintended situations. During a sunny outing to Southsea in August 1952, the Choir, 'owing to misunderstandings' arrived late for lunch at a watering hole but succeeded in gate-crashing a wedding reception, alarming the bride and groom! Compensating with a convivial evening at the Harbour Lights, Portsmouth, the coach party headed home but outside Winchester they picked up two 'mysterious passengers' who had missed their London train. By the time the man and woman (not of bride and groom appearance) got off the coach at Swindon, they still hadn't confessed, leaving choir members wagering they were an eloping couple or international criminals? *In vino veritas?*

During a separate Bournemouth trip, the Hon. Secretary well and truly 'disgraced himself', but with an amalgam of remorse and rebellion, he pleaded the Fifth Amendment. Some trips were smaller scale, by car, and few members owned a car in the 1950s, but they sang anyway.

In 1956 Mr A. Carr (a founding member) was presented with a commemorative 'Billiard Cue and Case' costing £3.10d, for dedicated service as Chairman. No-one was taken for granted.

The Choir's widening reputation and high standard of performance meant dependability. Audiences, satisfied with consistently dedicated, cheerful singers, often invited the Choir to return and entertain them again, as with the Cheltenham Welsh Society. Some of the most gratifying concert engagements were of the repeat prescription therapy. Choristers may have varied in their tastes for favourite (or least favourite) concerts, but there seemed to be unanimity of preference for the annual Battle of Britain week's Gala Concert organised by the Air Forces Association.

For seven years the Choir featured in this prestigious event, mostly at Cheltenham Town Hall and once at the Playhouse Theatre in 1958. On this occasion, the Dedication was voiced by Air Vice Marshal S.N. Webster, CBE AFC, a great admirer of, and friend to, the Choir. Appropriately, the Choir's programme included 'The Battle Eve' and 'Comrades in Arms', another example of the Choir's fraternity. It was always exhilarating to share the stage with great soloists, vocal and instrumental, bands and orchestras, including the Cotswold Orchestra. All concerts attracted large audiences. One poignant moment proved

Three wise men or three coins in a fountain?

'Voices from afar are calling' – Fred Dean (right) joins in the teasing.

'We told you to stop for petrol!' – Dave Williams, Frank Beagley and Norman Tansley (seated) playing truant from choir practice.

salutary for future performances. The audience call for an encore could not be honoured, as no encore had been rehearsed. Such disappointment was never repeated!

Camaraderie wasn't restricted to Smiths and the general community around the Choir's stomping ground of Bishop's Cleeve. Kindred singers were national in friendship. They became international in June 1972.

WANDERING MINSTRELS

Cheltenham's twin town in France, Annecy, is dominated by the photogenic splendours of the Haute Savoie Alps and Lake Annecy. In 1972, Annecy's principal choral society, the Harmonie Chorale, was celebrating its Centenary year. Links with Cheltenham's Twinning Committee resulted in an invitation from Harmonie Chorale to Smiths Industries

Battle of Britain week.

Choir assembly outside
Cheltenham Town Hall in
readiness for the 1,300-mile
round trip to Annecy.

(Aviation) Men's Choir. Totally contrasting with a male voice choir, Harmonie Chorale had mixed gender voices, specialising in religious music under the direction of its Wagnerian-orientated conductor Marcel Dijoud. The Chorale had originally been founded under the influence of priests, although membership had been opened to the laity. In 1972 several abbés still sang with the Chorale, one of them blessed with a basso profundo voice the Smiths ensemble might have cheerfully kidnapped! And of course, there were all those lovely ladies too...

The Choir party comprised forty-three singing members, the Musical Director, special accompanist emeritus Jim Portbury (pianist extraordinaire) and guest harmonica soloist Brian Chaplin, a national champion and future Mayor of Cheltenham. Debut member Roger Western later became Mayor of Tewkesbury, as did an earlier member Cliff Burd.

A 'famous' Black and White coach conveyed the party to the channel ferry, then on the seemingly interminable overland trip to Annecy. Accommodation was shared between hospitable *en famille* lodgings and a spacious hostel, the Marquisats Youth Centre. The visit posed a cultural challenge; Harmonie Chorale didn't speak much English, the visitors didn't speak any French, with the exception of one choir member who trebled as tour correspondent, interpreter and concert compère. This gratifying role spawned new friendships and reunions that lasted nearly four decades (still in French), but music proved to be the international language.

After an initial civic reception at Annecy's Town Hall, including the Choir's informal impromptu performance 'in civvies', and a visit to Old Annecy, a conventional concert was staged at the Salle Pierre Lamy Theatre in town. The highly appreciative audience was enthralled by the varied programme of singing augmented by harmonica music and a solo reading, in French, of an Alphonse Daudet short story. The climax of the concert was a

Impromptu sing-song after the Mayoral Reception at Annecy's Town Hall. The top tenor section is off-camera. Note the distinctive fingertip direction of Dave Williams.

TTBB arrangement of 'Dem Bones, Dem Dry Bones', inspiring an enthusiastic standing ovation. Dave Williams, well wined and dined, was at his most dynamic, directing with unforgettable flair and passion. The 'Voice from the Valley' had come a long way. Three decades later, the Harmonie Chorale Director, Marcel Dijoud, was still rehearsing that memory of 'Dem Bones' right up until his untimely death.

The crowded 'afterglow' at the Brasserie de L'Hotel de Ville, lasted into the wee small hours, both choirs singing themselves hoarse with the encouragement of Pernod and beer. Next day the weary party relaxed during a visit to a local abbey, the site of its Saint, Francois de Sales, then a conducted boat tour of Lake Annecy. Stunning scenery, new comradeship, *entente cordiale*, and the Choir's debut trip in Europe, the first of many.

In 1973, the Harmonie Chorale reciprocated by visiting Cheltenham, their members travelling by sea or air. Reunited in London, they were escorted to Gloucestershire by some of their English hosts.

Lake Annecy, 1972.

Harmonie Chorale Choral Society, Annecy, with the Mayor of Cheltenham outside the Town Hall, May 1973, after the Civic Reception.

CELEBRITY CONCERT

VISIT
BY THE FAMOUS

HARMONIE CHORALE

OF

ANNECY

SATURDAY JUNE 9th AT 7·00 pm

AT

CLEEVE SCHOOL, TWO HEDGES RD

BISHOPS CLEEVE

ADMISSION BY PROGRAMME
35p INCL. REFRESHMENTS
15 p O.A.P's

Entente cordiale. Reciprocal concert by the visiting French choir from Annecy, accommodated *en famille* by hosts from the Cotswold Male Voice Choir, 1973.

Marcel Dijoud, Musical Director of
Harmonie Chorale, Annecy, and an eminent
tenor soloist.

An official mayoral reception and luncheon at Cheltenham Town Hall was a matinée for the evening concert in Bishop's Cleeve Comprehensive School. On their own breeding ground the host choir merged with a capacity audience, warming to the splendid, controlled singing of the Harmonie Chorale. The predominantly French and Latin religious programme included a delightful rendition in English of 'Nobody Knows'. In his beautiful tenor voice, the Musical Director Marcel Dijoud, respected throughout Europe, mesmerised the audience (especially Choir wives), accompanied by Arlette Girod.

At the convivial 'afterglow', listeners were entranced by the booming bass of Jean Birraux, an 'off-duty' French abbé, performing 'Ole Man River' in English, while nursing a powerful beer thirst as he travelled down the Mississippi!

During the next day's conducted Cotswold tour, camaraderie was cemented. In the home of Don and Joan Baker, one French soprano sang in celebration 'Unissons Nos Voix' - 'Let us Unite our Voices'. Harmonie Chorale departed in nostalgic mood. But as their coach filled, the singers spontaneously burst into a spirited farewell 'Ce n'est qu'un au revoir' – 'It's only cheerio, we will meet again' - to the tune of Auld Lang Syne. A seminal cultural exchange was complete, setting a template for future tours. Harmony was achieved, fellowship earned. The Entente was definitely Cordiale.

John Dodds was principal organiser for both exchanges.

BROADCASTING

The Choir's first broadcast was from Standish Sanatorium but, during the vinyl era, it made several recordings in mono and in stereo. The first was a two song seventy-eight rpm ('Arabella' and 'The Soldier's Dream') made in Gloucester, circa January 1954 during a snowstorm. Two extended play records followed in 1970 and 1971, providing useful studio experience for future television appearances. In 1974, the popular national contest

Record sleeve photographs from the 1970 and 1971 LPs.

Opportunity Knocks, hosted by Hughie Green, dominated the small screen. It was produced by Keith Beckett and was a musical challenge for the Choir.

Auditioning at Thames Television's Teddington Lock studios, the Choir competed with a wide variety of multi-talented artistes, ranging from pop groups like Gloucester's 'Witticombe Fair' to exotic dancers. Somewhere in between sexuality and solemnity, the forty-six strong Choir qualified for the Finals, singing with dash and dignity. On Easter Monday 1974, they were awarded third place in the national competition, adjusting well to the commercial demands of showbiz. A little camera-shy, the choristers had welcomed any chance of light relief at rehearsal time. During a tiring day of waiting and wondering – mostly being ignored by Hughie Green – they were requested to sing something other than their scheduled number. The Musical Director decided on the famous African tribal song 'Kumbayah'. Interpreting that as 'Come By 'Ere', Hughie Green declared 'You mean

Choir assembled at Smith's Industries main entrance before departure for a recording session in Birmingham, 1970.

that old Welsh hymn tune!' The Choir riposted 'on the night' by singing a sparkling rendition of the toe-tapping hit musical number 'Standing on the Corner, Watching All the Girls Go By'.

There were plenty of pretty girls going by in the studio, but that delightful distraction didn't detract from the Choir's disciplined performance. Fervour and finesse again. Opportunity had knocked, 'And I mean that most sincerely, folks!'

In 1976, the Choir competed in the HTV Television's mixed talent show, *Best in the West,* in Bristol. In an inter-county contest, Gloucestershire was represented by the Smiths Industries team of performers. Nearly fifty choir members progressed through the competition heats and sang in the finals, winning first prize. The winner's trophy was accompanied by a cheque for £100 to be donated to charity. Triumph was sweet, commercial success yet again contrasting with the arcane demands of yesteryear's

SMITHS' TEAM BEST IN WEST

A team from Smiths Industries, Bishop's Cleeve, won the final of H.T.V.'s Best-in-the-West competition, beating Clarks Shoes, of Street, Somerset, by 62 points to 58.

Fifty teams from Gloucestershire, Avon, Wiltshire and Somerset entered the competition which was run on a league basis for each county. The four league winners entered the semi-finals.

The competition consisted of a "Pop the Question" round, an "Eentertainment round which involved Smiths Industries Male Voice Choir, a "Remember This" round and an "On the Range" cooking round.

The Smiths Industries team won a trophy and a £100 cheque which were received by Mr. C. H. B. Barden, Marketing Director.

The money is to be given to a charity of Smiths Industries' choice.

1974 *Best in the West* clipping.

YOUR ITV   103   **WEST** **HTV**   **admit one**

to The Television Centre,
BATH ROAD,
BRISLINGTON,
BRISTOL BS4 3HG.

ALAN TAYLOR presents

"BEST IN THE WEST"

Doors open: 7.30 p.m.   No admission after 7.45 p.m.
TV Recording ends 9.15 p.m.

This ticket is complimentary and not for sale. No admission is possible after the time stated. Taking photographs during the performance is not allowed.

The management reserve the right to refuse admission without giving any reason.

NO CHILD UNDER THE AGE OF 16 WILL BE ADMITTED.

The company will not accept responsibility for the loss of clothing or any personal possession in the studio.

HTV *Best in the West* ticket, 1976.

ITV Studios,
Bristol, 1976.

music festival competitions. The photograph of a jubilant Chairman, Roy Abbott, flanked by Dave and Nan Williams, displays the gratification, accumulated through many years of serious rehearsal and passionate singing. In both television appearances, 1974 and 1976, Dave Williams' musical direction was charismatic and the Choir responded in kind.

Although singing was always taken seriously, there was never too much gravitas in the Choir community. Fellowship was fun, members' individuality always respected. The formality of platform deportment didn't camouflage the healthy humour of the Choir

'Gentlemen Songsters out on a spree?' From left to right, front row: Arthur Sheppard, John Cartwright, Alan White, Alan Gilkes, Dave Williams, Harold Price, Dewi Davies, Aled Williams. Back row: Phil Howells, Brian England, John Dodds, Dave Ford, 1977.

'Here's A Health to The King, And a Lasting Peace', King's Head Pilgrims. From left to right: Clive Williams, Albert England, Dewi Davies, Malcolm Williams.

comics like Jack Williams, who delighted audiences with his party piece, the eye twinkling raconteur cockney in flat cap, mac and scarf, a roll-up pinched between thumb and finger.

By contrast, Reg Dimond guaranteed laughter with his smock-and-straw character, who told jokes in Devon dialect. Sometimes 'dressing up' sketches were performed by a volunteer squad of singers (not transvestites, of course) to provide salutary comedy. Johnny Parker and Stan Moxom were two choir comedians who were always in tandem, apt to improvise fun as twin court jesters, a kind of medieval 'dynamic duo', sometimes over the top, yet still memorable. There were also colourful compères; in different decades the concert MC might mask his natural urge 'to act' while ensuring that the programme ran smoothly. Cyril Cox was an early memorable compère, but no member ever enjoyed playing the role with more pleasure than John Cartwright. His meticulously prepared introductions and stage asides evoked Shakespearian theatre, amusing audiences and, to quote a wistful baritone member, 'Giving the boys a breather between numbers!' Teasing was never far away from the singing.

EN PASSANT

Informality was favoured for AGM venues. However rigid an agenda, the setting would be the relaxed atmosphere of a hotel in Ledbury, Upton-on-Severn, Tewkesbury, Painswick or Worcester, with a buffet supper (and maybe a drink or three) afterwards. Doing business didn't mean doing penance. Likewise, committee meetings weren't restricted to severe surroundings. Eventually, the no-smoking, drink-drive, breathalyzer culture proved beneficial to the throats of serious singers.

Practice nights became sacrosanct, to most members an inviolable date on the weekly calendar. Rehearsals gravitated from the factory to other locations: Prestbury, hotels in Cheltenham, a church hall, and the Labour Club in the Royal Well. The Choir had no political affiliations or cultural discriminations, totally neutral in the cause and love of music. A man was accepted for his singing voice - and his sense of humour.

An enthusiastic Welshman (North Wales, of course) proudly brought his well-travelled mother to Wednesday practice at the Labour Club. 'Well, Mam?' he asked afterwards, 'How did we look?' She replied sternly 'Like rows of ****** Toby Jugs, boys!'

So many years and so many soloists within the Choir. Many would-be soloists were given the opportunity to prove themselves on stage. Some took early retirement and returned to the ranks. One or two took offence - and relocated themselves elsewhere. The 'founding fathers' of the Choir produced some exceptional soloists. William 'Griff' Griffiths and Gwynne Jenkins regularly sang solo, their contrasting tenor voices also often blending effectively in duet, most memorably in the mood-changing 'Watchman, What Of The Night' and 'The Bold Gendarmes'. They and their duets symbolized the great variety within the Choir ensemble.

Unforgettably, John Rees (eldest of four brothers) was blessed with a bel canto tenor voice fine enough to grace the greatest of opera houses. Other members, maybe too shy to sing solos in public, were the basso profundo singers Colin Jones and Arthur Bateman, sadly not members at the same time. Harold Kenyon was the sweetest of Irish tenors. John Dodds, the mellowest of baritones, was memorable for his solo 'Kumbayah' (but not the Hughie Green version!). Synonymous with 'Shenandoah' and, especially, 'Kalinka' was Gerry Moran, the Wearside soloist who sang the Siberian-style song with such panache that he was quoted in the local press as 'that worthy Cossack from the snows of Durham!'

MATURITY AND EVOLUTION

Years passed, the Choir matured to a membership of over fifty, and only a small percentage of singers still worked at Smiths. From its parochial beginning with internal factory participants, it now attracted engagements alongside Desford Colliery Band,

The Royal Gloucestershire Hussars, RAF Innsworth Band, Burton Constructional Newhall Band and, of course, Churchdown and Gloucestershire Police Choirs. Fellowship was sealed, but less insular now. 'Let no clamour rudely pealing, disturb the strain melodious...' So choristers had long been happy to sing as 'Comrades in Arms', but it was time for change.

As Smiths Industries (Cheltenham) Men's Choir, it still qualified for Company subsidies, but executive officers still had to be Smiths employees. An alternative was to sever affiliation to Smiths, lose its financial grant and change its title. Such drastic action would have once seemed unthinkable, even disloyal. But the runes had been cast. An Extraordinary General Meeting was held on Wednesday 21 July 1976, at 7.30 p.m. 'to consider and if thought fit,

Presentation to Dave Williams, 1977. Six of the 'Founding Fathers', from left to right: Fred Dean, John Haggett, Ken Eldridge, Dave Williams, Bill Griffiths, Gwynne Jenkins. Chairman Alan White is behind Nan Williams.

Given at the presentation, the inscription reads 'DAVE WILLIAMS, FOUNDER AND CONDUCTOR, 1949 – 1977, FROM HIS FRIENDS, THE COTSWOLD MALE VOICE CHOIR, 2 FEBRUARY 1977.'

to approve the first motion that the name of the Choir be changed to the 'Cotswold Male Voice Choir', with effect from 1 January 1977.

Thus it was. Only the name changed. In the context of the new constitution, it wasn't re-incarnation. It was the same choir but re-christened. The members who objected to this alteration sadly resigned from the Choir. So, under its title the Cotswold Male Voice Choir, Dave Williams conducted the Choir for his final concert, at Shaftesbury Hall, Cheltenham, on 27 January 1977.

The programme included favourite songs; 'Morte Christe', 'Speed Your Journey', 'Close Thine Eyes', the irrepressible Gerry Moran splendidly sang his solo in 'Kalinka'. Enid Walklett soared almost into orbit, Dave Williams was at his consummate best, one listener marvelling rhetorically 'How can one man control so many men so well?' The audience was mesmerised. The mood was joyful yet poignant. Band and Choir combined in the fitting finalé, 'Comrades In Arms', but the resonating climax was the haunting Dvorak music and the most appropriate of farewells 'I'm - a - going - home...'.

END OF AN ERA

On 2 January 1977, Dave was ceremoniously presented with an inscribed solid silver cigarette case in honour of his retirement. His ever-supportive wife Nan, a great friend of the Choir, received a crystal rose bowl. A biographical ballad, especially written for Dave by Second Tenor Dewi Davies, still resounded from Dave's sixtieth birthday celebrations. The farewell party, full of high-voltage emotion, typified the long established camaraderie of the Cotswold Male Voice Choir. The tears and the drink flowed; the singing and cheering seemed endless.

Later, again in the homely reassuring atmosphere of the Labour Club, accompanist Jessie Gott was presented with her inscribed retirement silver salver. Between them, Dave and Jessie had devoted forty-six years of music-making to the Choir. This was the end of an era, the passing of a local legend.

The old saying 'Conductors are born, not fabricated' applied perfectly to Dave. He accepted the challenge of starting a choir on a factory floor, once recalling how exciting it was getting men who normally don't sing at all, to sing together, in harmony. The harmony was social as well as musical, resulting in fraternity, an ensemble of singers lasting at least sixty years. Almost an entire generation of singers has passed since May 1949, leaving an honoured legacy for its current membership.

Revering pitch, tone and musical instinct, Dave soon dispensed with his conductor's baton, preferring dynamic fingertip direction, a smile rather than a frown. His inspiring leadership reflected his total devotion to the Choir's welfare. Although undoubtedly 'father of the Choir', he never referred to it as 'my choir'; it belonged to the membership, the original eighteen singers having increased to fifty-six. Some of his fine qualities remain unsung, but during twenty-eight years of selfless service he conducted nearly 350 concerts and 1,400 rehearsals, without any honorarium. To adjust a quotation from the poet Coleridge, for Dave, 'Music is its own exceeding great reward.'

He rarely missed a concert or practice night. There was no officially elected deputy Musical Director during his era. There were so many special moments in twenty-eight years, yet Dave specified one. When conducting 'Steal Away' for the first time in concert, an audience member stood up during the applause then, during silence requested 'Sing it again. Please!!!' The Choir obliged.

From the Welsh valleys he'd brought *hwyl* and *hiraeth* to the wolds of Gloucestershire. When he retired to Ystradgynlais in 1977, he 'came home', bringing with him treasured memories of fellowship. His choir tenure may never be surpassed. His memory endures today. Dave's ashes are scattered on his beloved Black Mountains, overlooking Swansea Valley. His devoted wife Nan's ashes are scattered there too. 'The Long Day Closes.'

Above left: Bristol Eisteddfod Winners certificate, 1963.

Above right: Merit certificate from Kingswood and District Eisteddfod, 1965.

Left: Merit certificate from Cheltenham Festival, 1969.

Boulevard Style on Cheltenham Promenade. Harmonie Chorale singer Anne-Marie David with Dave Williams, 1973.

'Once more our journey begins.' Rear view of Les Neale, extreme left. Profile of John Cartwright, just off centre right. Departure from Cheltenham Town Hall, May 1973.

(Left) Ken 'More Tea' Mortimer discussing musical accidentals with Fred Dean (right) in profile. Is Bill Samuels (wearing the sheepskin coat) leaving the stage already? Coach departure from Bishop's Cleeve, May 1973.

Top left: Alan Donnelly (left), John Dodds (centre) and Fred Dean (extreme right). Coach departure from Bishop's Cleeve, May 1973.

Top right: 'Once more it's time to be moving.' New camaraderie established. John Dodds is on the extreme right. Cheltenham Town Hall, May 1973.

Centre left: Dewi Davies, of 'And the church clock struck eight!' fame, seems tempted to depart with the Harmonie Chorale. Cheltenham Town Hall, May 1973.

Centre right: Annecy visitors, May 1973. Harmonie Chorale President Pierre Guy next to Nan Williams. Madame Guy is on the extreme left.

Left: Fond farewells. 'Ce n'est qu'un au revoir!' Departure time for the Harmonie Chorale overland travellers, May 1973.

Silver Jubilee Celebrations, Carlton Hotel, Cheltenham, 1974. Ladies from left to right: Mrs Brunsdon, Mrs Davies, Mrs Williams (Jnr) and Mrs Williams (Snr).

1949 – 1974

SI

THE
SILVER JUBILEE DINNER
OF
SI MENS CHOIR

CARLTON HOTEL
CHELTENHAM

FRIDAY, 3rd MAY, 1974

7.30 for 8 p.m.

Bar Extension to 1 a.m.

Ticket to the Silver Jubilee Dinner, 3 May 1974.

Mr. C. H. B. Barden (left), marketing director, Smiths Industries, presenting a cheque for £100 to Major ⸺ Hoddinott, regional organising secretary, mid-west region of the Arthritis and Rheumatism Council for Research during a ceremony at Smiths factory, Bishop's Cleeve, yesterday. The money was the prize won by the Smiths team in the TV Best-in-the-West competition. Fourth from left is Mr. Alan Taylor, compere of the show, and fifth from left Mr. C. J. E. Hosegood, director and general manager of Smiths Industries. Looking on are members of the winning team.

HTV *Best in the West* award, 1976.

Mr. G. E. McWatters, vice-chairman H.T.V., presents the Best-in-the-West trophy to Mr. C. H. B. Barden, marketing director, Smiths Industries. Looking on are Mr. D. Franks, captain of the Clarks team, and the compere of the show, Alan Taylor.

SMITHS' TEAM BEST IN WEST

A team from Smiths Industries, Bishop's Cleeve, won the final of H.T.V.'s Best-in-the-West competition, beating Clarks Shoes, of Street, Somerset, by 62 points to 58.

Fifty teams from Gloucestershire, Avon, Wiltshire and Somerset entered the competition which was run on a league basis for each county. The four league winners entered the semi-finals.

The competition consisted of a "Pop the Question" round, an "Eentertainment round which involved Smiths Industries Male Voice Choir, a "Remember This" round and an "On the Range" cooking round.

The Smiths Industries team won a trophy and a £100 cheque which were received by Mr. C. H. B. Barden, Marketing Director.

The money is to be given to a charity of Smiths Industries' choice.

HTV *Best in the West* award, 1976.

The television performance which won HTV's prestigious *Best in the West* award, 1976.

'Lights, camera, action!' HTV studios, 1976.

HTV's *Best in the West*, 1976.

Scenes of the Choir during HTV's *Best in the West*, 1976.

Retirement party, 1977.

COTSWOLD MALE VOICE CHOIR

Annual Dinner and Dance

at

Tewkesbury Park Golf and Country Club
Lincoln Green Lane, Tewkesbury

on

Saturday 9th December, 1978

Dancing from 9 pm. to 1 am. to **'The FORTUNE'**

Reception 7.30 pm.
Dinner 8.00 pm.

Ticket £5.00
Dress optional

Ladies Night ticket, 1978.

A fan from Japan during the interval of a concert near Evesham, 1980s. This charming Japanese lady is 'monitored' by Harry Butcher (rear left) and Glyn Owen (rear right).

An afterglow dignified by three ladies, Cath Hall, Mary Moran and Nicki Stillman, 1980s.

PART TWO

1977-1999

A COTSWOLD SONG

A rare blend of two eras. Shortly after his retirement from the Cotswold Male Voice Choir, founder conductor Dave Williams attended the 1978 Cleeve School concert, directed by his successor Leslie Burgess. The only occasion when the two men were pictured together, they flank Jean Lea, accompanist, escorted by two of the 'founding fathers', John Haggett

Founding Musical Director David Williams (second left) with Jean Lea and Leslie Burgess (second right), the only occasion they were photographed together, 1978. (Photograph by Mike Charity)

On stage at Bishop's Cleeve School, 1978. (Photograph by Mike Charity)

and Fred Dean. Bishop's Cleeve, the original birthplace of the Choir, provided homes for dozens of choir members. Note the 'Castilian Elegance' of the line up.

Dave was soon succeeded by the superlative Leslie Burgess. There was no official handover from one Musical Director to another. A very short inter regnum period was supervised by the gallant Arthur Sheppard, who had conducted rehearsals and a couple of concerts. He was also crucially involved in the writing of the Cotswold Male Voice Choir Constitution, with effect from January 1977. Arthur is also fondly remembered for an afterglow incident at a hostelry in Lechlade when, homeward bound from a choir engagement, he generously offered to play the pub piano, as rare accompaniment to 'The Gentlemen Songsters', and add some decorum to the ambience. Arthur nobly struck only a couple of chords before the piano (yes) collapsed!

New to the male voice stage, Les Burgess had noticed the newspaper invitation for a replacement Musical Director auditions to be held at the Cheltenham Labour Club. His potent music instincts encountered some self-questioning. Happily his doubts evaporated in the unstinting encouragement of his wife Morfydd. From a shortlist of potential musical directors, Les was accepted by the Choir with 'open arms, hearts and minds'. A new era had begun.

Les inherited nearly three decades of choir tradition, experience, pride, and the compassionate generosity of its members. Choir fellowship was relayed to him with a musical, if metaphorical, baton. He absorbed it readily, so continuity was assured. The Choir absorbed his individuality, responding to his own personal style and refinement. To the very extensive library of music he added a fresh outlook. Not only did he arrange other composers' music, he composed his own songs too. Much later, in 1998, Cheltenham Arts Council awarded him with their prestigious Music Award and he was overall winner of the Joyner Cup.

As a boy he was taught to play the cornet and trumpet. During National Service in the Army he was an instrumentalist in the Staff Band of the Royal Tank Regiment, and also in other military bands. A student at the Royal Military School of Music, Kneller Hall, he was an instrumental prize winner and a fanfare trumpeter. Later, as a civilian, he performed in theatres in the north of England and played assistant solo cornet in Morris Motors Band, under the direction of the famous Harry Mortimer.

Returning to his native town of Cheltenham, he immersed himself in its cultural life, playing principal trumpet in the main orchestras of the area. In the 1970s, he formed his own flourishing Brass Consort, and also the Cotswold Consort Orchestra. This latter ensemble shared concerts with the Cotswold Male Voice Choir, raising funds for charities at venues including Cheltenham Town Hall and Gloucester Cathedral.

As the Deputy Head of a Cheltenham junior school, Les was ever enthusiastic in his encouragement of music-making and general musical development of students and young people. He organised hundreds of local school children to perform public concerts in aid of charities, especially to help the Disabled Association.

His strong influence over the spread of music proliferated, typified by the Cheltenham Youth Brass, whose director's baton he passed on to a former youth member, thus perpetuating a musical togetherness that matured into adulthood.

A versatile composer and lyricist, Les wrote a special musical entitled 'A Cheltenham Celebration'. In 1988, three hundred local children performed this musical presentation of the town's history to commemorate the regency visit of George III three hundred years previously. Other compositions by Les were performed on radio and television. Then came 'The Cotswold Song'.

Early in his incarnation as Musical Director, Les composed the music and wrote the lyrics to his most appropriate of pieces, 'The Cotswold Song', which he dedicated to the Choir. It was an instant success and has since remained the popular signature tune. Even nowadays, long after his retirement from the Choir, Les appears by special request to direct his song in concert, as conductor emeritus. It is also associated with long-serving piano

Two delightful ladies of the Choir: Jean Lea, accompanist (left) and Enid Walklett, soprano (right) flanking Musician, Mayor and Minister, 1978.

accompanist Jean Lea, who first played it on its public debut, and regularly afterwards. Jean and Les 'arrived together' and remained in tandem, with distinguished success, maintaining the Choir's high standard of aspiration and attainment.

Already familiar as accompanist to, and sometime duet singing partner of, soprano Enid Walklett, Jean was a respected piano and organ teacher. Organist at Holy Trinity Church, Slad, she was in demand as a piano and organ accompanist to vocalists and instrumentalists throughout the Cotswolds, sometimes playing solos herself. A skilful, sensitive accompanist for the Choir, she performed faithfully, without flamboyance, inspiring confidence in all the singers. Husband Peter sang in the Choir. Their son Steve was often a guest conductor, accompanist and soloist, accomplishing each role with distinction. Such a musical family, invaluable to the Choir.

Les Burgess directed the Choir in multiple venues in distant places, including Stratford, Birmingham, Coventry, Gloucester, Hereford, Holland, Bavaria, Ebbw Vale (twice), etc. But perhaps his favourite engagements were in his home town, Cheltenham. Through his musical and military connections, he activated the popular annual December joint concert, shared with the Band of the Lifeguards, Household Cavalry, in Cheltenham Town Hall. It was a spectacular engagement, always commencing with four Fanfare Trumpeters in plumed helmets, the entire band resplendent in ceremonial scarlet and gold uniform. Band brass, percussion and woodwind contrasted dramatically with the male singers, performing to an entranced capacity audience. This mutually respectful fellowship was an 'annual fixture' anticipated with pleasure, never disappointing. But despite the professionalism and organisation onstage, it was impossible to legislate against the unthinkable – a bomb scare!

STOUT-HEARTED MEN

In 1991, the annual joint concert already in progress, local police alerted performers and the 800 members of the audience to a tip-off security warning. Quickly the Town Hall was evacuated. Most of the bewildered audience were gathered outside, seeming suddenly deprived of their evening's entertainment. But the Choir remained in formal line-up outside the Town Hall determined to keep singing. And so they did, disciplined and professional, mostly without overcoats on a midwinter pavement, honouring the old theatrical axiom 'the show must go on'.

Surrounded by the grateful crowd of listeners, Les Burgess, in white dinner jacket, conducted the Choir in an al fresco concert, without accompaniment, until it was safe to re-enter the building. The concert ended indoors with most of the audience intact. A unique event, it proved that the Cotswold Male Voice Choir was equal to any unpredicted challenge. In James Bond parlance, it might be said that the ensemble was 'shaken, but not deterred!'

A bomb scare at the
Town Hall, 1991.

STAGE MANAGEMENT

The offstage drama of the Guards concert was an ironic reminder that there could be onstage theatricals too. Good stage management was always an essential requisite of public performances, needing vision, skill, planning and fortitude on the part of the stage manager. Dignified platform deportment ideally complemented the music being performed. Without instruments to tend, singers have only themselves to discipline, taking care to concentrate on the musical director, and their own singing. But occasionally that proves ingenuous, a stage manager's nightmare.

At a Wilden Church concert in the Midlands, the Choir was on stage, well managed, well rehearsed, singing respectfully in such a hallowed place. Nearly half-an-hour into the singing, a Welsh member, Dewi Davies was poised to declaim an introduction to 'Eli Jenkins' Prayer' by Dylan Thomas. The words were spoken clearly with dramatic emphasis 'And – the – clock – struck – eight!' As if on cue, the expectant pause was interrupted by boom, boom, boom as the real church clock began striking – yes, eight! Petrified at first, the audience started to snigger. Choir members grinned, hesitated, then singers and listeners bonded in shoulder-shaking mirth. The concert was a success.

During a joint-concert rehearsal at the Colston Hall, Bristol, the duty Musical Director stopped the singing and exhorted the assembly, 'Sing with more passion, my lovely boys! Don't you have passion in your lives?' Choir member Phil Hall stood up straight to the riposte, 'Not since this morning!'

Mischievous gremlins have been blamed for another stage nightmare. One April Fool's Day, the Choir was booked to sing at the Rose's Theatre, Tewkesbury. During afternoon rehearsals the members took their seats on stage, closely monitored by the stage manager plus the theatre manager. Neatly in place, the singers were about to do a warming–up song when the back row of the staging collapsed. The entire rear row of members disappeared backwards.

Horrified onlookers held their breath – until a solitary hand appeared over the back of the stage. A bald head, then another hand materialized, then slowly, all hands and heads, in a mountain climber's routine, were reunited in view. The theatre manager, jaw on a loose hinge, appealed to Don Baker, who was stage manager that day,
'Fantastic! As it's April Fool's Day, do you think you could keep that bit in as part of the act tonight?'

'Well, yes' Don replied 'if you can arrange to have some ambulances standing by!' The staging later proved to be secure and therefore 'all right on the night'. There were no casualties but that farcical afternoon accident was nicely redolent of an old Chad cartoon, 'Wot – no stage?!'

Another unplanned stage incident happened at one of the regular concerts at Cleeve School. Always a popular engagement, the Choir was at ease in familiar surroundings with a welcoming audience. The vigilant stage manager guaranteed regimented ranks of

On stage once more at Bishop's Cleeve School, 1978. (Photograph by Mike Charity)

singers – with one exception. Master of Ceremonies was John Cartwright, affectionately nicknamed Captain Mainwaring. A very serious programme announcer, he introduced the delightfully poignant song 'The Old Woman', and was so moved by the lyric that he insisted on reciting the words before the Choir sang them. 'As a white candle, in a Holy place...' After a recitation worthy of a RADA audition, John solemnly returned to his place in the front row, bowed to the audience, sat down. And his chair collapsed! While the disrupted front row was realigning, a choir comedian muttered, 'It's the Roses Theatre again, only back to front!'

A further 'stage business' crisis took place on the world-famous stage of the Royal Shakespeare Theatre, Stratford-upon-Avon. Participating in the prestigious Grand Gala Variety Show Festival '78, the Choir were due to perform the finalé of drama, dancing and music entertainment. With time to relax before the evening show, some members retired to the renowned Dirty Duck Inn (more evocative than the intended Black Swan). There, they religiously lubricated their throats in preparation for some dedicated singing later –

a 'pre-glow' rather than 'afterglow'. After discussing 'lives of the luvvies since the Bard's day', the boys returned to the theatre.

Serious business, Festival '78 was organised by the South Warwickshire Stage Society to raise funds for St. John Ambulance. The theatre acoustics were so exquisite that even a subtle stage whisper would project to the furthest balcony. A much beloved choir member, Gerry Ryan, had been steadily 'lubricating' throughout the day. He had an awkward gait caused by a metal leg, so was prone to stumbling. By performance time scores of artistes, including many young children, were assembled backstage. It was nerve-racking enough waiting to sing before 1,200 people in the holiest of holies. But muttering, mellow Gerry unnerved everyone by tripping, falling into the curtain, then bellowing a ripe Irish expletive (unprintable here) that defied the 'SILENCE PLEASE' sign. Shakespeare may have chuckled; the stage manager was not amused, but theatrical stage-fright assumed a double identity that evening. The Choir performed with distinction, including the then popular song 'The Floral Dance'. So here's a toast to all those long-suffering stage managers, including Phil Howells, Pete Wilkes, Walter Blewitt, Phil Hall, Colin Mort, Dennis Watson et al. Thank you, gentlemen.

SAD LOSSES

Dewi Davies loved singing, and humorous ballad writing. When visiting the famous opera stage at La Scala, as a tourist, he was invited to test the celebrated acoustics there. 'Sing something appropriate' a guide coaxed him, 'Think of the great tenors'. After some angst of indecision, Dewi took a deep breath and began serenading to the gallery 'Just one Cornetto, from Walls Ice Cream...'

Dewi sang in his final concert at Bristol, loving every note, still singing on the choir coach on the way home to Tewkesbury. Sadly, during that night, he died, at peace, and ever remembered.

Another popular choir singer was the top tenor Charles Davies. Even before joining the Choir, Charles was a much respected and experienced soloist. His rich, mellow voice was suited to venerable songs such as 'The Holy City', but he is arguably best remembered for one of his favourite pieces 'Goodbye', from The White Horse Inn. He sang it regularly when performing with the Choir. In fact, it was the final solo he ever sang.

After a formal dinner at the Bell Inn, Eckington, choir members and their partners mingled socially, enjoying the warmth of chat and laughter. Inevitably there was impromptu singing, Charles standing up to perform his beloved 'Goodbye'. He sang it with his usual panache, delighting his listeners. It was exquisite timing. Almost straight away, Charles collapsed. Despite the ministrations of doctors and nurses, who were present that evening, Charles did not recover. The sad irony of his passing endured in the haunting refrain of his final song, still revered in the memories of his brethren.

Charles Davies Memorial, honouring the bittersweet finale of a beloved singer, 1996. Increasingly, the Choir sings at the funerals of its members; camaraderie at its most meaningful.

FURTHER TRAVELS

Choir membership had steadily spread throughout the Cotswolds and beyond, some dedicated singers travelling, always at their own expense, from Worcester, Eckington, Tewkesbury, Evesham, Winchcombe, the Wolds, Oxford, Gloucester, Berkeley, Stroud and Painswick. As an ensemble, the Choir travelled further, linking with other choirs in Basingstoke, Cornwall, etc.

It was always good to reunite with multiple choirs at joint concerts with the English Association of Male Voice Choirs in Three Counties' abbeys and cathedrals. But the Choir particularly enjoyed its own tours outside the U.K.

In 1984, Bavaria represented the Choir's second European tour (a big gap since its Annecy trip in 1972).

Through the auspices of Tewkesbury Borough Council, the Choir were invited to visit the Miesbach area of Bavaria. The party, including soprano soloist Morfydd Burgess, travelled in two groups, one by air, the other by Luxury Castleways coach, reuniting in picturesque lakeside Schliersee. Accommodation was provided in a fairytale Gast Haus environment. The Bavarian Highlands beguiled the visitors with the splendid combination of Alps, forests and thoroughly 'green' areas. The famous atmosphere of Bavarian well-being was reflected in the local chalet-style houses, beautifully painted with national costume and hunting scenes, characterized by proudly, precisely stacked logs, in readiness for the wood-burning, porcelain-clad stoves. Baroque rococo church architecture, onion domes and bucolic landscape entranced the Cotswold visitors, as did Mozart's birthplace Saltzburg, during a daytrip into Austria. The gothic city of Munich was stark in contrast.

Guests were warmly welcomed by their Bavarian hosts, dressed in traditional clothes, the Hausham alpine 'Gluef Auf' adopted almost as an expletive! Daytime exploring included impromptu Choir performances in a local church and grammar school, in a 'Gymnasium', the glass-topped area creating sharp acoustics and indoor/outdoor ambience.

During a visit to idyllic Fischbachau the Choir attended, and performed unofficially, at a local wedding reception in a huge hall. Enjoying the hospitality of the gourmet wedding

Logs and Murals in Miesbach, 1984.

Hardly 'The Three Tenors' – not very good but cheap! In the background is the star of the show, Lake Schliersee.

'Guys and gals' by Lake Schliersee.

Impromptu sing-song in gymnasium area during a guided tour.

This has been a wonderful trip – thanks to the hard work done by people like you –: – Thank you, Dave –
Les Burgess

Wonderful Memories of a supremely Happy Tour! Morfydd Burgess – with love!

Die wunderbaren Tage werden wir nicht so schnell vergessen.
In Freundschaft Bernd Osku
Bruno Seyfried Tegernsee

MR & MRS John Joyce
Maureen.

Zur Erinnerung an sehr schöne Tage der Freundschaft
Heinz Krebs Tegern MV

Good Luck
John Dodds
J. Peljak
G. Peljak

it's all been said.
Jim Slater

A Wonderful Visit
Holloway

Jim Fleming.
Arthur Sutherland
Peter Hudson
Walter Blewitt
Derek Dolman
Fred Kinder
One of the "bachelors" les Neale.
"Wonderful" Mike
Malcolm Williams
Dick yn Fawr!
Albert Etchany
& Richard

Von wenigen Minuten schon
tief beeindruckt – schon
bald in England!
Schliersee, 28.5.84
Andreas Klein

[Page of handwritten signatures on a dinner menu, including names such as Cyril Palmer, Sam Ager, Bernard Strick, Glyndwr Owen, greetings to David, Rudi Vitus, "Pfundig is' gwesn!", WUNDERBAR, Phil Hall, Ted Booker, J. I. Davies, P. D. Bale, and others.]

Nocl viel Spaß beim Singen

all luck to you
and thank you very much
for coming!
Peter [_____] 28.5.84

Konrad [_____]
Ludwig [_____] Tegernsee

All the tour party and friends signed the dinner menu.

party Bavarians, the visitors were mesmerised by the celebratory dancing. Couples, young and old, spun around dizzily to the infectious beat of an 'Oompah Band', pausing only occasionally to change direction and spin round again, without variation. But there was no panel of dance judges, all the ladies graced traditional costumes with plunging necklines – and the bride wore black!

Cable car trips up and down Wendelstein Mountain were more sobering. More solemn was the official visit to nearby Lake Tegernsee, its city originally founded as an eighth-century Benedictine abbey. The Schloss served as an impressive venue for the Choir's joint concert with the local Lieder Kranz Choir. Although a rapturously received performance, there was still more musical climax at the Sunday morning service in a cloistered, cathedral-like church. In the ambience of incense, piety and ecclesiastical awe, some of the enraptured worshippers confessed, after the Choir's rendition of 'The Name of the Lord is Blessed', that they'd had to control their urge to break into delighted applause. No need for 'afterglow'. And when the visitors were finally driven away from Schliersee, idyllic sights and sounds disappeared as if from a fairytale – but not from memory.

Tour organisers were John Dodds and Dave Ford, CMVC.

CHOIRS COMING TOGETHER

In June 1982, the Choir combined with seven other male voice choirs in a joint concert at Cheltenham Town Hall. The evening's entertainment was planned to raise funds in aid of CLIC (Cancer and Leukaemia in Childhood). It was also the inaugural concert of the English Association of Male Voice Choirs (Western Division). This Association resulted from multiple choirs convening in the Severn Sound 'On Air' competition, and from the vision of several West Country singers aware of the need for blending separate choirs in public performance.

Previously there had been no organisation in England to compare with the established Male Voice Association that thrived in Wales, a kindred fraternity across the River Severn. The Association's constitution clearly aspired 'To foster and promote the enjoyment, fellowship and interest in male voice music in all its aspects'.

Since its inception, the Association's membership has expanded steadily, and the inaugural concert was an unqualified success. The guest soprano soloist was Morfydd Burgess, wife of Leslie, who became a regular and highly valued guest artiste with the Cotswold Male Voice Choir.

Participating also in that enhancing fellowship were the Bream, Churchdown, Drybrook, Dursley, Filton, Hereford Police and Malvern male voice choirs. These same 'Comrades in Arms' were equally successful in November 1982, when combining with the Band of Her Majesty's Royal Marines, in 'Tribute to the Task Force', at Hereford

Cathedral. Honouring the many casualties sustained during the Falklands War, the concert proceeds were shared by the Hereford-based Special Air Services Regiment and Hereford-connected HMS *Antelope* Dependants' Fund. Despite that bitterly cold night and tight security, the Cathedral's capacity audience warmed to the splendour created by the talents of skilful bandsmen and singers – a moving tribute to the Task Force. The concert was recorded as an EP for posterity. Singing continued afterwards in the SAS HQ. What a gig!

Subsequently, the Choir enjoyed regular reunions with kindred choirs at massed-voice engagements in Stroud, Worcester Cathedral, Gloucester Cathedral, Pershore Abbey and Tewkesbury Abbey, and is scheduled to again be the host choir in the 2010 concert.

During several decades of the Choir's incarnation, many 'outsiders' have been drawn to it, helping, but above all sharing. There have been guest conductors, stand-by conductors and stand-in conductors since 1977. Similarly, guest accompanists and deputy conductors from other choirs have all enjoyed that common choir quality – welcome. Likewise with guest soloists, vocal or instrumental, the Choir is renowned for its welcoming warmth. Even in a town hall tri-choir concert shared by Cotswold, Churchdown and Gloucester Police Male Voice Choirs, welcome was the word, compatibility rather than confrontation amongst friendly rivals. But fraternity does not exclude the ladies, who were ever received with grace and gratitude, soloists like Morfydd Burgess.

Morfydd participated in the seminal English Association of Male Voice Choirs' joint concert at Cheltenham Town Hall and, during a long association with the Choir, was part of that special family atmosphere welcomed at venues throughout the Cotswolds. Occasionally she shared a duet with choir member Albert England, but mostly she was a solo performer blessed with a beautiful Welsh soprano voice and an elegant stage presence that enhanced any concert in which she appeared. She sang on radio and television, and accomplished a successful tour of South Africa for a multi-racial charity. A specialist in traditional Oratorio, she was also at ease with First Performances by contemporary composers, though the great names Mozart, Beethoven, Fauré and Mascagni remained essential to her personal repertoire. Altogther she sang in nineteen operas.

Singing solos since the age of six, she won a scholarship to study with Joan Gray, Professor of Singing at the Royal College of Music, and later with Nell Moody of the Welsh National Opera. No stranger to the male voice choir circuit, she sang with Pontardulais and Stevenage choirs, as well as with the three local choirs mentioned earlier as guest soprano in the 1984 Life Guards Concert in Cheltenham Town Hall. Well remembered for her depiction of operatic characters like Susanna (Marriage of Figaro) and Santuzza (Cavalliera Rusticana), roles in Gilbert and Sullivan and musical comedy, she once performed a sweet and unforgettable solo of her husband Leslie's own composition, 'Gently Open the Door' from the pulpit of Gloucester Cathedral. It was a magical, musical moment.

Waiting for the coach bound for Nottingham, outside the Cheltenham Town Hall, 1984.

Cheltenham Town Hall has always figured importantly in the Choir's development. As a central assembly point of departure for choir trips away it represented a familiar and reassuring landmark. The accompanying photograph demonstrates how well-groomed the members appear even in casual, liveried sweaters, contrasting with formal stage attire. Here the line up typifies happy choristers prepared to travel anywhere for the joy of singing. A hearty chorus preludes a tour of Nottingham, scheduled to perform at St Helen's Church, Burton Joyce, then at St Sampson's, York.

By contrast, the adjacent photograph depicts the singers in concert dress, standing behind the Town Hall for formal grouping, as ever with 'Castilian Elegance'. Choir imagery was

The Choir at the Imperial Gardens, Cheltenham, 1985.

never better captured than at the annual joint concerts, each December, with the Band of the Lifeguards, regular engagements that spanned the years between 1983 and 1998. Spiralling costs terminated this popular 'fixture' between uniformed bandsmen and civilian singers, when acquaintanceships were so enjoyably renewed.

But the typically gratifying portrait shown on page 93 encapsulates the mood and motive of the 1989 joint concert. Choir Musical Director, Leslie Burgess, a former Fanfare Trumpeter, and Peter Lea, Choir Chairman, hand over two cheques for £1,000 each to the grateful representatives of the Cystic Fibrosis and the Riding for the Disabled charities. Looking on respectfully are Fanfare Trumpeters, Band of the Lifeguards. It also distinguishes between professional musicians and amateur singers, yet both are united in music-making, subordinate to money-making.

'Stout Hearted Men' and a courageous lady. Choir rehearsal in Prestbury, 1963.

Cleeve School annual concert in the early 1960s.

Cleeve School annual concert in the early 1970s.

The Choir, suitably angelic while singing in Church, 1970s. No thought of the 'afterglow', of course!

Munich. Illustration from the beer menu of the Alpengasthof, 1984.

Sacred and Secular Songs. The Choir performing in Church, Moselle tour, 1998. The tour accompanist is Jane Harper, assisted by Dot England.

The Altar Boys. A 'stage aside' by Leslie Burgess has them amused. Moselle tour, 1998.

'Tenor and baritone' duet. Albert England, top tenor, and Bill Taylor (a profound bass 'in real life'). Moselle tour, 1998.

Tourist guide, Lake Tegernsee, 1998.

'Afterglow', Moselle tour, 1998. Bruce Rhodes (far left, now retired Life Member) looking as if he has entered into the 'spirit' of the occasion, an elegant and eloquent compère.

'Afterglow' singing, an unstoppable force once the beer is flowing, Moselle, 1998.

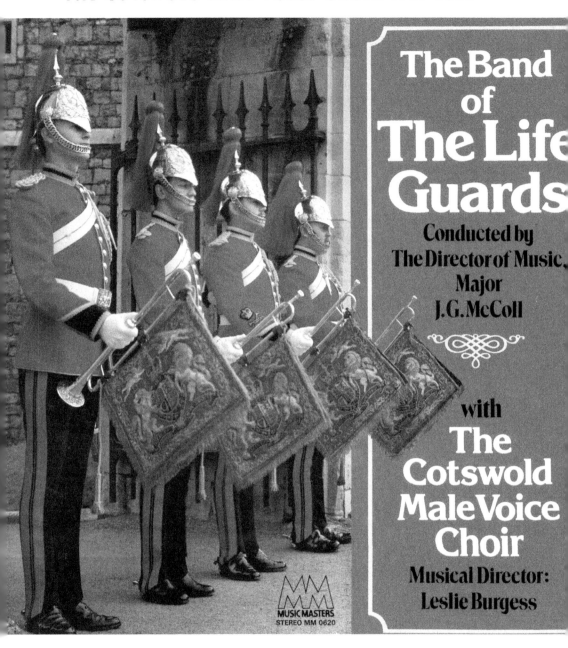

The Band
of
The Life
Guards

Conducted by
The Director of Music,
Major
J. G. McColl

with
The
Cotswold
Male Voice
Choir

Musical Director:
Leslie Burgess

MUSIC MASTERS
STEREO MM 0620

The Life Guards Concert LP from 1985, recording the tradition of a fifteen year partnership.

Opposite top: Band of the Life Guards, annual version of Scarlet and Black, 1989.

Opposite bottom: Band of Life Guards. A musical collaboration of amateurs and professionals for two charities, 1989. Four Fanfare Trumpeters look on as Les Burgess, a former Fanfare trumpeter himself, presents a cheque.

Programme for Pam Ayres at the Town Hall, 1990. The famous performance poet complements music by local songsters.

The 1998 joint concert marked the coming-of-age of Leslie Burgess and Jean Lea, Director of Music and Piano Accompanist, both simultaneously achieving twenty-one years of discerning, dedicated service to the Choir. During that tenure the Choir also entertained Flowers Band and an ensemble from Russia at the Town Hall. Wonderful memories...

SPECIAL GUESTS

Some famous soloists guested only once at choir concerts, including the popular Pam Ayres. But her singular performance produced multiple memories of the Town Hall's special atmosphere. Pam Ayres was a household name at the time of the Choir's December 1990 joint concert. A common experience linked choir and poet; both had appeared on the popular television show *Opportunity Knocks*, in 1974 and 1975 respectively. Both resided in the Cotswolds, an affinity reflected in the evening's performance. The internationally respected poet's stage recitation of her own comic verses delighted a full house, compatible with the Choir's choice of programme. Singing travelled to the bar afterwards. Leslie Burgess' catchy arrangement of 'Mary's Boy Child' was seasonally welcomed. Soloists Charles Davies, Albert England and Haydn Sutton, another beloved booming bass who ranks with the best of soloists in the star 'cast list' of the Choir, ensured that the boys weren't totally upstaged by a lady. A lovely start to Christmas!

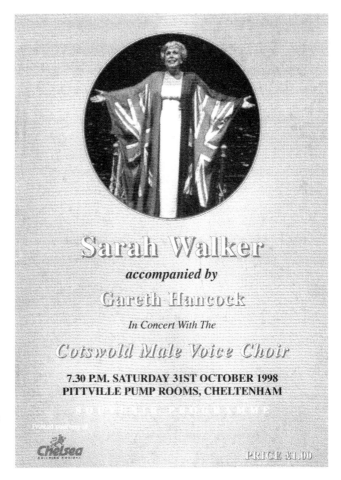

Sarah Walker programme cover, 1998. International diva forsakes the world operatic stage to sing in her home town with the Cotswold Male Voice Choir.

Another 'one-off' guest appearance with the Choir was personified by the world-famous diva Sarah Walker. The Cheltenham-born opera singer, who had performed with stars like Luciano Pavarotti, forsook the Royal Albert Hall spotlight to sing in Cheltenham's Pittville Pump Rooms. Although vividly remembered for singing 'Rule Britannia' at The Last Night of the Proms in 1989, attired in a Union flag dress, Ms Walker was formerly a Pate's Grammar School for Girls pupil, who used to sing with Cheltenham Bach and Christ Church choirs. Once conducted by Leonard Bernstein, the Prima Donna was happy to sing in her home town, backed by the Choir rather than an orchestra. William Taylor's bass solo in 'Battle Hymn of the Republic' was stirring, almost in 'Rule Britannia' mood. This concert, in October 1998 just preceded the December concert of the Life Guards, both acknowledging the joint twenty-one year tenure of Leslie Burgess and Jean Lea. Such 'one-off' engagements remain priceless.

Group photo taken in Ebbw Vale, 1998.

THE CHOIR ON THE ROAD

Most concerts are performed indoors, usually in halls, theatres, schools, colleges, citadels, army barracks, cathedrals, abbeys and churches – whose hallowed acoustics are usually a favourite with singers, an exception being Gloucester Cathedral's 'delayed' reverberations. Singing on homeward bound coaches has a unique licence. Marquee singing has its own peculiar ambience, halfway between indoor and outdoor. But the Choir has often sung al fresco; formally, as in the garden festival atmosphere of Ebbw Vale (twice), Hyde Park, Pittville Park, Cardiff, Hailes Abbey, for ATV Television, when 'In A Monastery Garden' was sung after a twenty-five-year choir gap. Informally, fun and relaxation have occurred on board an evening river cruise along the Avon from Tewkesbury; on a Sunday afternoon cruise on a river in Cornwall; a tour on Lake Annecy in France. Open air and open vowels aren't always compatible, but a lusty sing-song is usually therapeutic. In this informal category another example might be the late-night serenading of muddied members outside the Dog Inn, near Gloucester, maintaining harmony as they struggled to extract the carolling tenor Peter Fahy from the rose bed. 'Kyrie Elision!'

And so to Holland, from 3 - 7th April 1991, the choir party travelled in two groups, by air and by land, similar to the trip to Bavaria. Linking with the Hague based König Male Voice Choir, the visitors performed their main formal concert in a grand church, but also gave an impromptu performance at the Amstel Law Courts. Based in hotel accommodation at Lisse, the Choir enjoyed visiting the famous and spectacular Keukenhof Tulip Garden Centre.

Tour organisers were Dave Ford and Ted Booker, CMVC.

Cardiff Arms Park
World Choir logo,
1993.

The Choir first sang in the temple of Welsh rugby in 1992 with Tom Jones and Dame Gwyneth Jones, returning in 1993 to be a component of the much publicised World Choir of 10,000 voices drawn from Britain and abroad, performing at the famous Cardiff Arms Park to a capacity crowd. Special guest soloists included Welsh tenor Wynford Evans and international singing star, Shirley Bassey. It was a unique experience. Tenby in 1994, represented another visit to the Principality, the 'Land of Song'.

During a long weekend in September 1995, forty choir members travelled to Dublin to participate in the Voices of the World massed, mixed voice choirs at Landsdowne Road. Over 4,000 voices were recorded in concert by Telecom Eireann R.T.E., including choirs from UK, Ireland, Canada, Ukraine, Poland, Finland and France. Unified in song, accompanied by the National Symphony Orchestra conducted by Geariod Grant, this global choir included two of Ireland's soloists, soprano Suzanne Murphy and tenor Tonan Tynan, plus Italy's Cesare Zamparino and Paulo Kudriavchenko from Odessa.

In October 1996 the Choir visited Cornwall to link with the English China Clay Industries' Male Voice Choir at a successful concert in aid of a Children's Hospice, when almost £500 was raised. During this visit the Choir met up with old friends from the Rame Peninsula Male Voice Choir. The Cheltenham/Rame exchanges had become an important relationship between 'stout hearted men', linked by song, in concerts staged in contrasting parts of the country.

One notable Rame reminiscence is that after a Cheltenham church concert, the 'home team' gratefully devoured genuine Cornish pasties brought by their visitors from Cornwall. T'was enough to inspire a chorus of 'The Floral Dance'!

Similarly, the Choir's links with Basingstoke Ladies Choir resulted in mutually enjoyable concerts at venues in their respective towns. Camaraderie welcomes exchange but knows no boundaries. Other musical marriages include ensembles like Tredegar Town Band, Wolverhampton Orpheus Male Voice Choir and the popular Flowers Band, the band of the Gloucestershire Constabulary and The Salvation Army.

THE HAPPY WANDERER

Music is ever mobile, the Choir still meandering across the map of Europe. After France, Bavaria and Holland, Germany beckoned to the minstrels. In May 1998, they lodged in the Hotel Lellmann at Löf, situated between Koblentz and Cochem in the Moselle area, renowned for its grapes. Predictably, the thirsty travellers relished a wine-tasting session in a Bierkeller at the Briedel Haus hotel. Good for the vocal chords, of course, enhancing the singing at various venues, including the Baden Neuenahr town hall, where the revolving stage created indoor and outdoor acoustics, post London Palladium era!

Social pleasantries included a ceremonial exchange of memorabilia between the Mayor of Trier and Mayor of Gloucester (represented by the Choir), during which the visitors

The Methodist Church, Basingstoke.

Moselle tour, 1998. A true troubadour, Don Baker seems to be impersonating Al Jolson, but Morfydd Burgess (extreme left) doesn't seem to be convinced.

were presented with appropriate T-shirts. The formal concert was shared by the Cotswold Choir and the Pfalzel Male Voice Choir, held in a church in a village suburb of Trier. Post-concert celebrations were traditionally lively, as suggested in the accompanying photographs. Inn or church, any atmosphere is always receptive to the Choir's repertoire of sacred and secular songs. Singing suits the situation…

Tour organisers were Dave Ford and Harold Spindler, CMVC.

THE COTSWOLD SONG

Mozart's museum house is also a sacred shrine attracting countless pilgrims. But it is still alive. The great master's presence resonates through the building. Passing reverently, in silence, through the music area, away from kitchen and bedchamber, the visiting Cotswold Male Voice Choir entertained their own private thoughts. Mozart's old piano was tantalizingly mute, almost daring someone to play a forbidden chord. Close by was a specimen Mozart original manuscript, protected in a glass case. Magnetic!

Leslie Burgess lingered there, gazing down at the precious, faded ink notation. His expression was rapt, awed, his silent homage discouraging any disturbance. Beneath the glass cover there was – life. Nearness. The mighty Mozart seemed almost inhalable, and this sacred voyeurism spanned centuries. Leslie may still revere that special moment a quarter century ago. It was part of the Choir's visit to Bavaria; music made it happen.

Leslie brought discerning direction to the Choir. He'd inherited a unique 'sound', especially the much admired tone and diction, and he refined it. Like his predecessor, he conducted adult male singers with flair and charisma. Occasionally he played trumpet solos 'to keep the lip in shape', but he also shared his considerable skills of TTBB music arrangement and composition. He believed that 'songs are poems set to music', and he proved this.

Ralph McTell's renowned 'Streets of London' responded famously to TTBB arrangement, popular with singers and audiences. Likewise the evergreen 'Mary's Boy Child', so captivating for listeners, so compulsive for performers.

'The Bells of Heaven' composition resounds each Christmas and New Year, while 'Hand Me Down My Silver Trumpet' is demanding as well as satisfying to sing. A much requested song, 'I Want to Say to You' has proved suitable for any occasion, its charming tune and romantic lyric guaranteeing its international appeal. For Cotswold appeal, Leslie's arrangement of the much admired Johnny Coppin poem 'This Night the Stars…' is peerless, a marriage of lyric and music unlikely to fade.

Aforementioned, 'The Cotswold Song' retains a permanent place in the Choir's repertoire and in the hearts of its singers. Composed in dedication to the Choir and first performed in Warden Hill Church in October 1978, it was used as the theme tune for *ATV Today*, in 1979, a programme featuring Cotswold scenes. Recorded live in concert

Coppin's Christmas

package

With carols, songs, stories,
and poems from the Cots-
wolds, Sunday promises to
be an evening full of local
flavour.

Coppin is well known for
his Gloucestershire songs as
featured on BBC 2 TV's
"Song of Gloucestershire"
programme, and his album

"Forest and Vale and High
Blue Hill".

Since then he has released
a follow-up album "English
Morning" which includes
three seasonal songs which
are proving popular —
"Christmas Eve" (words by
John Drinkwater), "Forest
Carol" (by Leonard Clark),
and "Winter" one of Frank
Mansell"s Cotswold Ballads.

Accompanied by Paul

Burgess and Geoff March,
Coppin will include these
and several new carols and
songs associated with
Gloucestershire and the
Cotswolds in the concert.

Having just completed
recording an LP with Laurie
Lee, the celebrated writer
from Slad, Coppin has asked
him to read some of his
powerful poems — such as
"Village of Winter Carols",
and "Christmas Landscape"

which capture so beautifully
the spirit of a country
Christmas in the Cotswolds.

In the middle of a busy
schedule of concerts, the
Cotswold Male Voice Choir
find time to make a guest
apperance. They will sing
several seasonal songs and
carols and an arrangement
of Coppin's "This Night the
Stars" by their conductor
Leslie Burgess.

Paul and Jane Burgess
will play delightful recorder
duets, while Ken Langsbury
will amaze with his Cots-
wold stories, all delivered in
his unique style!

The concert is being held
at Cheltenham Town Hall,
starting at 8pm.

Cheltenham News cutting, 1988. A favourite with choir and audience, Johnny Coppin's regionally-
evocative song 'This Night the Stars' was arranged for TTBB by Leslie Burgess.

Leslie leaves on high note

I t started out as a two-year job. But when Leslie Burgess stepped down recently as musical director of Cotswold Male Voice Choir, he could look back at a tenure of 22 years.

Mr Burgess, a trumpet player, auditioned for the job in 1977, when his wife heard that the choir needed a new leader.

He bowed out after the choir's Christmas concert at Cheltenham Town Hall and has handed over the reins to Tony Richards from Greet, near Winchcombe.

His two decades in charge have seen the band perform with people like poet Pam Ayres and Cheltenham-based novelist Sue Dyson, who is also a mezzo soprano singer.

⁀   were also more dramatic highlights. Mr Burgess forged a lin̲ ̲ ̲ years ago with The Band of the Lifeguards and they now play an annual charity concert at Cheltenham Town Hall.

"I decided to take the job for something to do and thought I'd stay for a couple of years. But when I got there the atmosphere was so good, I got into it and I ended up staying," said Mr Burgess.

"The job is to take practices and to plan the programmes and decide the music. I wrote some pieces myself.

"One of the first things that I wrote after a year was a piece called *The Cotswold Song*. That was very successful and we recorded it.

"It was used on a programme about the

Outside the Town Hall in 1991

Cotswolds on ITV and I was told that it even turned up on a television programme in Africa. I've often wondered what it was used for."

O⁀ ⁀oncert sticks in mind more than most. In 1991, when the ch̲ ̲ ̲d the band were due to perform at Cheltenham Town Hall, a security scare meant that the entire audience of 800 people had to be evacuated before the performance even started.

"We thought we were going to lose the audience, because people were drifting off," said Mr Burgess, who lives in Warden Hill with his wife Morfydd.

"We started singing in the street and most of the crowd stayed, we only lost a few."

He said that he will maintain close links with the choir and enjoys the get togethers after a show.

"We all arrange to meet up in a pub and then the singing carries on. I can tell whether it's a two pint song or a three pint song, depending on how well they sing it. They always seem to perform one of my songs, *I Want To Say To You* and that's always nice to hear."

The choir's secretary, Tony Richards, said: "Les has been a brilliant musical director. Part of it is to do with his passion for all types of music as well as his musical ability.

"He really had a great insight into the way that a song should be sung properly and the feeling that you should put into it. He believes that songs are poetry put to music and we should sing the words as they were written."

Sarah Maybank

Picture: Jessica Horner 200420/18

Leslie Burgess, and below, at the Garden Festival, Wales

Leslie Burgess retired as Musical Director in 1999.

at Winchcombe Methodist Church, it was later synchronised in 'silent filming', with the Choir moving through the evocative ruins of nearby Hailes Abbey. This lilting song was recorded separately at St Luke's as a memento of the Cotswolds, for local folk, and for overseas visitors to take home as a 'souvenir in sound'. It is a reminder that the Choir is rooted in the Cotswolds, yet its reputation has steadily spread far beyond its geographical boundaries.

When the Labour Club became too small to accommodate an expanding choir, alternative rehearsal premises were needed. After a few experiments, the Choir settled comfortably for some years at Highbury Church Hall, then in the grand atmosphere of Dean Close School. This prompted jest like 'Where Shall I Be?' and 'Thou Gavest', but it was a truism to claim that the 'Rhythm of Life' had accelerated since the formative years of the Choir, although the title 'I'll Give You Hope' always applied in the singer/audience equation. From brewery drayman to High Sheriff of Gloucester, choir membership represented a comprehensive cross-section of society. Whoever, wherever, however, whenever, the members always posed the question – why ever? Surely the answer has always been, 'We convene and commune because we love singing.'

Thus it has been for fifty years. Members die, but hopefully the Choir will never perish. The fraternity endures because music endures. And Leslie Burgess had invested twenty-two years of his life in maintaining that 'Hand Me Down My Silver Trumpet' remained after his retirement.

Amazingly, the Choir never commemorated its Golden Jubilee. Perhaps its sixty year anniversary celebrations will atone for this. But for half a century the Choir survived and thrived under the charismatic musical direction of just two conductors. This remarkable statistic is now registered in choir lore. Successive members hold a temporary stewardship of the Choir, and policy is in the eye of the beholder – or in the ear of the listener?

As an adult I have deeply personal reasons for being grateful to choir members for their great generosity and kindness. Yet my respect for them started in 1949 when, as a ten-year-old boy soprano, I sang alongside them the solo *Calon Lan* (Pure Heart), at a Cheltenham concert. I revere all the pure hearts of the men I've known since then, hundreds of singers with diverse backgrounds, and with hundreds of songs. I fancy that if we are all reunited eventually in another place, bonded in fraternity by the love of singing, then there may be one large cosmic choir, well directed, in harmony, at peace. And the universe will be a better place.

PART THREE

WRITTEN BY STEVE ALLSUP

1999-2009

A DECADE OF CHANGE

It is at this point that I have to hand over the narrative to other current members of the Choir, whilst still keeping control of the authorship, spirit and tone of this history. Where better to start than the current Chairman's Christmas letter to the Choir, dated 13 December 2008, on the eve of the Choir's sixtieth anniversary?

Dear Choir,

I was a little surprised to learn recently from Malcolm Williams (Life Member and son of our founding Musical Director) that the fiftieth anniversary of the Choir in 1999 passed without celebration. I did not join until 2001, so I was unaware of this. What a different and more

Choir role: Brian Blessed

Blessed role for Brian

SHAKESPEAREAN actor Brian Blessed is to be the figurehead of a West male voice choir, it emerged last night.

Well known for his loud voice and being a talented singer, Blessed jumped at the chance to become the honorary president of the Cheltenham-based Cotswolds Male Voice Choir.

The choir had been drawing up a shortlist of celebrities they could target to help raise its profile. The idea of inviting Blessed came to the choir's chairman Steve Allsup after watching the actor perform as Pavarotti on a TV show.

Within a matter of days Blessed wrote back and said "How can I resist?".

Although he will not be asked to sing regularly with the choir, Mr Allsup hopes he will come along to one of the fundraising concerts.

Actor Brian Blessed kindly agreed to accept the appointment of Honorary President in 2004.

confident choir we must be today because our sixtieth anniversary next year is certainly not going to go unnoticed.

2008 has been a successful and very busy year. By the time we meet for our last engagement of the year on New Year's Eve we will have completed twenty-three events. This was commented upon at our last E.A.M.V.C. meeting in Worcester. I was asked 'Aren't your members worn out?' and 'How did BetFair find you to sing at Twickenham?' To the first question, I was able to answer that our attendances at most events this year have been higher and, as for the second question, the answer was staring them in the face. How did they know so much about what we were doing if they weren't all looking at our website?

On the subject of singing at Twickenham, my thanks go to all the members who attended. It was a huge commitment. I wish those who did not make it to Twickenham could have been there to see the effect our music had on the thousands who heard us. I can still see the sad, cold faces being transformed into smiles and laughter as they approached our staging. Please also extend our thanks to your partners and families for 'lending' you to the Choir for up to fifteen hours on three consecutive Saturdays.

Although our star is rising in terms of morale, recruitment, publicity, bookings and finance, I would not want us to lose sight of our primary reason for singing together. Whilst enjoying ourselves, we mainly support local good causes at local events. This is the heritage that has been passed down to us by the eighteen men who first met in the Smiths canteen in Bishop's Cleeve at 5.30 p.m. on 11 May 1949 (source – Malcolm Williams), and by every member who has been part of our choir since.

My personal thanks must go to our musical department and to our committee for their unquestioned support. In Martin, Geoff, Roy and Rosemary, we have both an efficient and talented team. Apart from one person, our committee comprises members who have joined in recent years. This is to our advantage, in that they can look at the Choir subjectively and none are afraid to ask 'Have we thought about doing things differently?' It is not my usual style to single out individuals but, on behalf of the whole choir, I want to thank our Stage Manager, Dennis Watson. He is always there at concerts well before the rest of us, having previously visited the venue to check that all is satisfactory, and he is always the last to leave.

My best wishes to you all for the festive season. 2009 is going to be a year to remember. Enjoy it!

Steve Allsup

CRISIS AND CONCERN

In 1999, if the Choir had thought that Leslie Burgess' retirement and replacement was going to be as seamless as had Dave Williams' retirement in 1977, they were in for a bit of a wait. This process was to take nearly five years, during which time two 'permanent' appointments would turn out to be 'temporary'. If a choir had to pick situations it most disliked, instability would be one of the top contenders. A choir without musical direction has no direction at all, and this is detrimental to morale.

A lack of morale is followed by lower member attendances at rehearsals and concerts. This was to become clear in the following years. Had it not been for the support of other conductors, the Choir may well, in the words of long standing members, 'have gone under'. These 'saviour' conductors included George Taylor (Gloucester Police Male Voice Choir), John Blenkinsopp (Churchdown Male Voice Choir), Steven Lea (son of accompanist, Jean Lea) and Michael Power. Michael was later to become Musical Director for two years but, at this time, serving as a Gloucester councillor precluded him from making a full time commitment.

It is a testament to their dedication and tenacity that the officers of the committee Albert England and Barry Foley (successive Chairmen), David Ford (Secretary), and Harold and Eileen Spindler (joint Treasurers) kept the Choir's wheels turning. As future officers were to discover, finding replacement conductors, often at short notice, is no easy task because talented conductors are in high demand.

However, during these years of turbulence, the Choir was still able to stage successful performances, so there was hope, but, while there was no musical direction it was not possible to introduce new music to the repertoire. No choir wants to be labelled as 'always singing the same old programme'. One member went so far as to declare 'If we ever have to sing "Vive L'Amour" or I have to hear "Kalinka" again, I am leaving.' They both appeared on the musical programme just a few concerts later and, true to his word, he resigned.

Although the committee and dedicated members worked hard to 'keep the show on the road', it was impossible to disguise discontent within the Choir's ranks. To address

Chairman from 2000 to 2002, Barry Foley (front left) in rehearsal with fellow bass, Colin Francis, 2003. Just behind is Paul Hipkiss, later to become Secretary.

On stage in Ireland.

this, it was decided to appoint a musical sub-committee tasked with 'advising' the musical direction of the Choir. This turned out to be unworkable and, following some bitter musical differences and clashes of personality, led to further fractures in choir personnel.

This became too much to bear for some members and people started to leave. Once this started, it drew others away and numbers in the Choir dwindled to fewer than thirty members by 2002. But the Choir carried on staging successful performances, so all was still not lost.

ON THE ROAD AGAIN

In 2001 and 2002 the Choir toured to Ireland and Germany respectively. The Choir's timing could not have been worse, for the 2001 tour to Cork coincided with the terrible attack on New York's Twin Towers. In a mark of respect for the victims, every establishment had closed its doors. The potential audience at the main weekend concert assumed it too had been cancelled, so the Choir was just about on its own in the performance hall.

One does not wish to make light of such a tragedy but two stories did come back with the Choir. In the concert venue, a gentleman had been laid out to rest in mourning, leading to murmurs of having a 'captive audience'. During the afternoon wait prior to the concert, the Choir soon found all hostelries to be shut also – well, almost. Killing time by walking around Cork, four enterprising choir members were sure they could hear noise coming from a 'curtains drawn' pub. Gingerly they knocked on the door which duly opened. In what must have looked like an 'Is there any room at the inn?' scene, they were welcomed and sang for their beer for the best part of the afternoon.

The 2002 tour to Germany was a familiar trip for the Choir members and, in their usual hospitable manner, the hosts made everyone most welcome and old friendships were renewed. There seemed to be an air of optimism on the Choir's return, but further crises were looming. Was the Choir's fortune ever going to change for the better? The answer was 'Yes', but not for some time.

During this turbulent time, there was one undoubted positive. On the retirement of Jean Lea, Geoffrey Mann agreed to the appointment of accompanist. Jean had been a wonderful accompanist and, to show the Choir's appreciation for her twenty-five years

Outside the hotel in Miesbach on the Choir's return trip in 2002.

Geoffrey Mann LRAM – what a talent!

of service, Albert England and other choir members travelled to her home to present Jean with a gift for her garden, which was another love of her life. Geoff took over but it was a few weeks before the piano music made its way back from Jean to the Choir. Undaunted, Geoff sight read the vocal musical parts and transposed the notes to the piano while the Choir rehearsed – as they would say today 'in real time'. To date, choir members are still commenting how lucky they were to replace one talented pianist with another.

2002 marked another hiccup in choir affairs. The newly elected Chairman encountered disagreements with the rest of the committee over the role of the Chair and the management of the Choir. He found himself in a minority of one and, taking the honourable course of action, he resigned but, to his credit, he remained and supported the Choir until the next year's AGM.

This meant that Steve Allsup, recently elected Deputy Chairman, had to step in as Acting Chairman. Nothing surprising about that, other than the fact he had only joined the Choir less than a year before. The previous full term incumbent, Barry Foley, had asked Steve to stand as Deputy Chairman saying 'Don't worry, it's only a nominal post and there's nothing to do but cover for the Chairman if he is away'. How prophetic were those words?

Despite problems, the demand for the Choir's services was still as high as ever. The number of concerts was still averaging over twenty per year, peaking at twenty-seven in 2003, when another sell-out concert was staged in Cheltenham Town Hall with Gloucester Police Male Voice Choir and the Flowers Band.

One of the Acting Chairman's earliest, and most unwanted tasks, was to tackle a situation with the then Musical Director's style. Choir members are used to a musical dressing down now and then from their leader, but only in a tone which recognises that all the members

Rococo Gardens Wedding Concert – The Choir started singing at weddings in 1959 and has sung at many funerals, especially those of its dear members.

are giving their time freely and often at some expense. Foot stamping and tantrums were not going to work. As a result, some members had already left and others were announcing their intention to do the same if things did not change quickly.

After receiving numerous telephone calls from the Musical Director crying off from rehearsals, often at very short notice, the Acting Chairman knew he had to act. One senior member of the Choir had commented 'He's had more absences in one year than Leslie Burgess had in twenty-two years!' Informing the Musical Director that his services were no longer required, the Acting Chairman announced to the Choir:

> I hope this is the only autocratic decision I ever make. I did not refer to the committee before making this decision, so they carry no responsibility. If you disagree with my action, I am content to step down and be a singing member of this choir, but (and this was the clincher) you will of course be volunteering, in future, to be the person responsible for finding a replacement conductor, usually with only a few hours notice.

Needless to say, no disagreements were aired.

Malcolm Williams, pictured with Michael Power (right) in 2006, is presented with 'Life Membership' of the Choir in recognition of his services.

This marked the turning point for the Choir because, with coincidental timing, Michael Power had recently informed the Choir he was standing down from his duties as a councillor and was looking forward to devoting more time to music. Apart from the appointment of Geoff Mann as accompanist, this was the only other piece of good fortune the Choir had had in a long time. There was now a truly talented and well qualified musical team in place and the Choir quickly settled down to some dedicated learning, including a new repertoire and Michael's own musical arrangements.

HAPPY RETURN

In 2005, the Choir returned to Cornwall, making new friends with the Praze-an-Beeble Male Voice Choir. Choir numbers had fallen to below thirty, but the twenty-two singers who travelled once again sang with style and were appreciated by a full church audience.

Idle hands get up to mischief. During the Saturday afternoon before the concert, tiring after walking around St Ives, a few members retired to the Sloop Inn for 'refreshment'. Within a short time, almost the whole choir and their partners were in attendance having a wonderful time. But where was the Musical Director?

Unknown to the rest, he had had to travel some miles back to the church, following an early rehearsal, to retrieve some medication. Time went on and the 'refreshment' flowed. Feeling some responsibility for delivering the Choir to the concert in a fit state to sing, the Chairman reminded everyone about their 'responsibilities', at which point the door opened and there was Michael asking 'I've had a terrible time finding that church. Who wants a drink?' It would have been mean to refuse!

In the 'afterglow' at the hotel after a successful concert, the Choir was joined by a number of the Praze 'boys'. Much jollity ensued culminating in bass singer, Haydn Sutton, standing to sing a solo. What an easy choice. We were in Cornwall. 'The Floral Dance'? Haydn launched instead into 'Glorious Devon'! Fortunately, Praze had a sense of humour, but they didn't join in.

The Choir consolidated during the next year and the occasional new member joined. Plans were made for two trips in 2006. One to York, at the invitation of the Lord Mayor, and the second to Annecy in France, at the invitation of Cheltenham Borough Council to celebrate fifty years of twinning between the two towns, a repeat of the trip made by the Choir to mark the twenty-fifth anniversary in 1972.

The York concert and weekend were very enjoyable with the Mayor and her Consort joining the Choir for dinner. Over coffees, the Chairman suggested that the Consort might like 'something a little stronger'. Making their excuses to the Mayor, the two made their way to the bar where they were soon joined by others and more impromptu singing followed.

Time off from singing – The Choir took a cable car up Mont Blanc in the Alps. The glacier is visible in the background.

THE FRENCH CONNECTION

A happy atmosphere continued for the next few months. This carried on to Bristol Airport while waiting for the flight to Geneva, then onward by coach to Annecy. Arriving at the airport with a couple of hours to spare, everyone was surprised to learn from member and tour organiser, Mike Wright, that he had 'negotiated a few good deals' and, as a result, we had all overpaid. He then proceeded to hand out cash refunds in envelopes to every member. Mike's health was toasted until the call to board was announced.

One thing marred this trip. Michael Power was unable to attend for medical reasons but, in the continuing good fortune of the Choir, Martin Dear had by then joined. Martin was an experienced chorister and choral tutor, and he agreed to conduct. Moreover, he was a French language teacher. What luck!

Considering he was a relatively new member and had only been asked to conduct at short notice, Martin carried it off with ease and the singers appreciated his relaxed style. Only Martin knows how he felt inside, but he looked the very picture of composure at the concert, which started with the Choir singing a French folksong 'Chevaliers de la Table Ronde'. In terms of musical appreciation, it ranks alongside the rhyme 'Sur le Pont d'Avignon' but it had the desired effect. The audience smiled, laughed and gave the Choir a standing ovation at the end.

Martin Dear, bottom right next to his wife Rosemary, fortifies himself before the concert.

Choir party outside Annecy's Town Hall.

On the Choir's return, and unforeseen, new questions now arose. Both Michael and Martin were very obviously talented musicians, so was it not possible to take advantage of both as musical directors? This seemed an innocent and positive question at the time but it was, once again, to lead to differences of opinions. Both parties were asked if they could find an accommodation which would allow them to 'share the baton'. Both agreed there should be no problem and that neither was worried about 'titles'. However, as the Choir had experienced after Leslie Burgess' retirement, someone had to be in charge.

The Chairman freely admits today that it was a misjudgement to allow this indecision to fester. As time went on, the pro-Michael and pro-Martin camps became more vociferous, even though they represented only a minority of the Choir. The 'Michael' camp asked, quite rightly, 'How can we abandon someone who came to the rescue of the Choir only two years ago?' The 'Martin' camp preferred his more laid back, but very well organised, style while still acknowledging their debt to Michael. It is important to note here that neither Michael nor Martin was responsible for this situation, rather other members' agenda.

Opinions went back and forth over several months and, without going into the more personal details, suffice it to say that the matter was resolved, sadly, by Michael's resignation. The Choir felt relieved that another divisive situation was over, but not before three other resignations and the continuing feeling by all that the matter could have been managed more honourably.

www.cotswoldmvc.org

Our website URL. A bold identity, a far cry from the Choir's shy infancy in 1949.

From that moment of regret, the Choir was determined and has gone from strength to strength. New members have joined, taking the choir roll into the mid-forties, of whom some have lent their professional expertise to the Choir by joining the committee. This is especially true with the Choir's 'marketing'. Sponsorship has helped some concerts. There is now a three man team working on publicity, resulting in numerous press and radio reports. The Choir's website, from which all enquiries are now generated, receives over a thousand visits a month. Out of these, more than half are new visitors who have never previously viewed the website. The Choir has a growing membership, finances are healthier than ever in its history, and the Choir's concert calendar is fully booked for more than a year in advance.

Bernard Stride (pictured) and Don Baker have been singing in the Choir from almost day one. A conservative estimate is that each has spent over 9,000 hours in rehearsals, concerts and travel. That is equivalent to over four full time working years. True commitment.

Those who have been members of the Choir for some time know that this success has not come about without cost, both emotionally and in terms of lost members. This goes some way to explain the commitment of the current membership, which is remarkable. In 2008, when adding up the concerts and wedding engagements (twenty-three), the rehearsals (forty-seven) and the committee meetings (eleven), more than eighty days have been accounted for by choir 'business'. And this brings us to the closing chapter of 2008, on the eve of the Choir's sixtieth anniversary…

SCORING FOR ENGLAND!

Towards the end of the summer the Secretary, Paul Hipkiss, received an email from one of England Rugby's sponsors asking if we would be willing to sing at Twickenham Station on the autumn international dates against Australia, South Africa and New Zealand. At first, the idea of singing on a draughty railway station did not appeal, but he and the Chairman did not know what they had in mind. However, it was a 'professional' enquiry and an equally 'professional' quote was emailed back. After all, this was going to be quite an operation involving coaches, multiple early morning pick-ups around Gloucestershire, fifteen hour days, food and refreshment throughout each day, setting up an outdoor PA system, arranging backing tracks and learning songs in Afrikaans, Xhosa and Maori.

The sponsors, BetFair, emailed back accepting the Choir's terms. Paul and Steve Allsup made arrangements to meet them in Twickenham and, only then, did they realise the scale of what was planned. Far from singing on a 'draughty' platform, BetFair had purchased the rights to the entire station of six platforms, all of which was going to be branded and the Choir would have dedicated staging erected.

The first Saturday came quickly and all the members boarded the coach, on time, at their appointed pick up places. So far, so good. The coach dropped off the Choir on time and it wasn't too much effort to get the PA system set up. Midday was approaching. This was the Choir's contracted start time. The first people they saw coming over the foot bridge from the platform were two very attractive girls wearing Australian shirts. The shout went up 'Okay chaps, this is it. One, two, three and… "Tie Me Kangaroo Down Sport"'. It was perhaps not the most musically challenging start to a choir concert but the humour was infectious with the crowd and choir alike.

There may have been a couple of technical hitches with equipment but, when they happened, the Choir carried on unaccompanied as though singing to 50,000 people was an everyday occurrence.

The next two Saturdays went equally well. The Choir became friendly with the railway staff and even dedicated 'The Bold Gendarmes' to the smiling members of the Metropolitan Police Force. Who says police men and women haven't got a sense of humour?

For three consecutive Saturdays both the Choir and 50,000 rugby fans per day braved the cold, but it didn't stop everyone joining in the singing … despite England losing all three matches!

The 2008 formal photograph of the Choir taken in their rehearsal rooms at Dean Close School. Third from the right in the third row is Don Baker, who was also in the 1954 photograph near the front of this book. What service!

At the end of the third Saturday, the Choir toasted all with some champagne (donated by the author of this book, bless 'im) and travelled home. On the coach, there was an air of disappointment that it was over, but a sense of relief that the Choir had pulled it off, with the congratulations of both the Police and the Events Manager of BetFair, who said 'It's the best entertainment we have ever staged in my time with the company!' If the volume of singing from the crowd and the increased visits to the Choir's website are a measure of that success, thousands of others from around the world agreed.

During the course of this narrative, there have been highs and lows but, fortunately, the former far outweigh the latter. The Choir has moved on, but a new crossroads is possible because the Choir's stock is high and it has become more 'professional'. But, to repeat the words of the Chairman in his Christmas letter:

> I would not want us to lose sight of our primary reason for singing together. Whilst enjoying ourselves, we mainly support local good causes at local events. This is the heritage that has been passed down to us by the eighteen men who first met in the Smiths canteen in Bishop's Cleeve at 5.30 p.m. on 11 May 1949, and by every member who has been part of our choir since.

If a second edition of this book is printed for the Choir's seventieth anniversary in 2019, perhaps we will find out if he was right.

'Castilian Elegance'. Even among so many singers and musicians in multicoloured atttire, CMVC are conspicuous. Birmingham Symphony Hall, 1995.

'Scarlet and Black' again. The Fanfare Trumpeters, Cheltenham Town Hall, 1990s.

The Bandmaster conducts both band and choir, Cheltenham Town Hall, 1990s.

COTSWOLD MALE VOICE CHOIR ROLL

1949–2009

Abbott, Roy
Abley, Ron
Acres, Richard
Adams, Alan
Adlam, Alex
Adlam, Sue
Ager, Sam
Aldridge, Ken
Allsup, Steve
Anderson, Alasdair
Andrew, Mike
Andrews, Bob
Andrews, Michael
Applemelk, Bruce
Ashman, Tom
Atherton, George
Attwood, Ivor
Attwood, Ray
Auld, Norman
Badge, Lyn
Bailey, Michael
Bainbridge, David
Baker, Don
Balster, Malcolm
Banyard, Steve
Bateman, Arthur
Baxter, Ted
Beagley, Frank
Beecher, Dominic
Best, John
Blackett, Graham
Blewitt, Walter
Bond, Neville
Booker, Ted
Booty, Tim
Bowden, Rod
Bowen, Judy
Bowers, Jonathan
Bragg, Mike
Brass, Mike
Bray, Chris
Brunsdon, Bill

Bruton, Keith
Burd, Cliff
Burgess, Leslie
Burgess, Morfydd
Burt, John
Butcher, Harry
Campbell, Bernard
Carr, Arthur
Cartwright, John
Cave, Brian
Clarke, Andrew
Connelly, Bill
Connop, Stan
Cook, Bob
Cooper, David
Cottle, Bill
Cowin, Nigel
Cox, Cyril
Clutterbuck, W.
Craven, Geoff
Crisp, E
Currie, John
Dainty, Norman
Dale, David
Davies, Charles
Davies, Dewi
Davies, Lyn
Day, Peter
de Gruchy, Peter
Dean, Fred
Dear, Martin
Dear, Rosemary
Dickinson, Kelvin
Dillon, Gary
Dimond, Reg
Dix, Graham
Dodd, Mike
Dodds, John
Dodds, Reg
Donnelly, Alan
Dougal, Doug
Dowsett, Jim

Draper, Peter
Dring, Jonathan
Eldridge, Ken
England, Albert
England, Brian
England, Dot
Ewing, Alby
Fahy, Peter
Febery, Terry
Fenton, Roger
Field, Richard
Fisher, John
Flemming, Jim
Flynn, Jamie
Foley, Barry
Ford, David
Foster, Jack
Foulkes, David
Francis, Colin
Gaul, Richard
Gaunt, Badger
Gibbons, Frank
Gibson, Bill
Giles, Stephen
Goff, Martin
Goodhall, Harry
Gott, Fred
Gott, Jessie
Gough, Ted
Grant-Hudson, Peter
Green, R
Griffiths, Griff
Griffiths, Hughie
Gunn, Phil
Haggett, John
Hall, Harry
Hall, Phil
Hall, Vic
Hanlon, Mike
Harris, Peter
Harvey, Richard
Harwar, Mike

Hawker, David
Hepburn, Richard
Hill, Mike
Hill, Terry
Hill, Trevor
Hipkiss, Paul
Holden, Bernard
Holland, Lew
Hollands, Robin
Hopkins, Russell
Howe, William
Howells, Phil
Hutt, Charlie
Hutt, Tim
Hynes, Matthew
Iles, Malcolm
Ingles, John
James, D
Jarvis, W
Jenkins, Gwynne
Jenkins, Reg
Jobborn, Adrienne
Johnson, Johnny
Jones, Arthur
Jones, Colin
Jones, D
Jones, Nick
Keane, Arthur
Kenyon, Harold
Kilminster, Pete
King, Charlie
King, Roy
Kirk, Bill
Lancaster, Jim
Lawrence, Clive
Lea, Jean
Lea, Peter
Lea, Stephen
Lee, John
Lee, Roger
Lewin, Dudley
Liggett, Iain

Luke, Derek
Lyth, David
Lyth, Jackie
Makin, Bill
Mann, Geoff
Manning, Ian
Mansbridge, F.
Marshall, Denis
Mason, Dave
Mason, Les
McCalla, Terry
McCarthy, ?
McCloy, John
McCullum, H
McDonnell, John
McGee, Alistair
McGreary, George
McKelvie, Alistair
Medlicott, Brian
Millard, Charlie
Miller, Dusty
Moate, David
Moran, Gerry
Morgan, Ivor
Morris, Ron
Mort, Colin
Mortimer, Ken
Moseling, Bob
Moxom, Stan
Munday, Jim
Munn, Richard
Neale, Les
Neville, Jeremy
Norman, Tony
Owen, Glynn

Palmer, Alan
Palmer, Cyril
Parker, Bill
Parker, Bryan
Parker, Johnny
Percy, Terry
Perrey, Bert
Pockett, Arthur
Powell, Graham
Powell, Mike
Powell, Tony
Power, Michael
Power, Stephen
Power, Tina
Price, Harold
Probert, Frank
Purcell, Graham
Rawlings, Gordon
Rawlings, Pat
Rees, Alan
Rees, Bryn
Rees, David
Rees, John
Render, Fred
Reynolds, Gary
Rhodes, Bruce
Richards, Tony
Rider, Reg
Ridge, Jim
Ridout, John
Robbins, Ken
Roberton, Norman
Roberts, Ken
Roberts, Mark
Ryan, Gerry

Salter, George
Samuels, Bill
Sheppard, Arthur
Skjonnemand, Bill
Slade, Freddy
Slater, Jim
Sloan, Dennis
Smith, Philip
Smith, Swin
South, Douglas
Sowerbutt, Ken
Sowerbutt, Murray
Spindler, Eileen
Spindler, Harold
Stafford, David
Stephenson, Nigel
Stevens, Lyn
Stillman, Colin
Stride, Bernard
Sutton, Haydn
Swift, Bill
Tansley, Norman
Tantum, George
Taylor, Andrew
Taylor, Bill
Taylor, Daniel
Taylor, David
Taylor, George
Teague, Graham
Thomas, Ian
Thompson, Ian
Thompson, John
Tomlin, Charles
Torboys, Charles
Tracey, Bill

Tracey, Joseph
Van Der Merwe, John
Viles, Cliff
Waite, Jim
Walters, Harry
Warner, Tom
Watson, Alastair
Watson, Dennis
Weir, Charles
Weir, Chris
Western, Roger
Whalley, Peter
White, Allan
White, Cedric
Whittaker, Duncan
Whittle, Tony
Wilkes, Peter
Wilkins, George
Williams, Aled
Williams, Cedric
Williams, Clive
Williams, David
Williams, I
Williams, Jack
Williams, Malcolm
Williamson, Simon
Wilson, Bert
Wilson, Peter
Wood, John (Jack)
Wood, Tony
Wornham, Jenny
Wright, Mike
and ...
?, Algie

Choristers, Musical Directors, Accompanists, Page Turners and Librarians
Total 306 members, as of 5 March 2009

Visit our website and discover thousands of other History Press books.
www.thehistorypress.co.uk